AUTHOR

Gabriele Malavoglia was born in Milan in 1989. After completing high school, he moved to Spain to continue his university studies, remaining on Iberian land even after graduation. Passionate about Italian and Spanish military history since childhood, he is a self-taught scholar and is taking his first steps in the field of publishing. He lives in Zaragoza and works as a logistics consultant for some local companies.

PUBLISHING'S NOTES

None of unpublished images or text of our book may be reproduced in any format without the expressed written permission of Luca Cristini Editore (already Soldiershop.com) when not indicate as marked with license creative commons 3.0 or 4.0. Luca Cristini Editore has made every reasonable effort to locate, contact and acknowledge rights holders and to correctly apply terms and conditions to Content.

Every effort has been made to trace the copyright of all the photographs. If there are unintentional omissions, please contact the publisher in writing at: info@soldiershop.com, who will correct all subsequent editions.

Our trademark: Luca Cristini Editore©, and the names of our series & brand: Soldiershop, Witness to war, Museum book, Bookmoon, Soldiers&Weapons, Battlefield, War in colour, Historical Biographies, Darwin's view, Fabula, Altrastoria, Italia Storica Ebook, Witness To History, Soldiers, Weapons & Uniforms, Storia etc. are herein © by Luca Cristini Editore.

LICENSES COMMONS

This book may utilize part of material marked with license creative commons 3.0 or 4.0 (CC BY 4.0), (CC BY-ND 4.0), (CC BY-SA 4.0) or (CC0 1.0). We give appropriate attribution credit and indicate if change were made in the acknowledgments field. Our WTW books series utilize only fonts licensed under the SIL Open Font License or other free use license.

For a complete list of Soldiershop titles please contact Luca Cristini Editore on our website: www.soldiershop.com or www.cristinieditore.com. E-mail: info@soldiershop.com

Title: **THE REPUBLICAN POLICE 1943-1945** Code.: **WTW-057 EN** by Gabriele Malavoglia
ISBN code: 9791255890980 first edition April 2024
Language: English; layout: 177,8 x 254 mm Cover & Art Design: Luca S. Cristini

WITNESS TO WAR (SOLDIERSHOP) is a trademark of Luca Cristini Editore, via Orio 33D - 24050 Zanica (BG) ITALY.

WITNESS TO WAR

THE REPUBLICAN POLICE 1943-1945

PHOTOS & IMAGES FROM WORLD WARTIME ARCHIVES

GABRIELE MALAVOGLIA

BOOKS TO COLLECT

CONTENTS

Introduction .... pag. 5

The Republican Police .... pag. 7

    Organigram .... pag. 14

    Armament .... pag. 15

    Fallen .... pag. 19

Public Security Inspectorates .... pag. 27

    The situation in German Operation Zones .... pag. 30

Armed Police Force .... pag. 43

    Autonomous Police Battalions .... pag. 43

    'San Giusto' Autonomous Legion of Public Security .... pag. 44

    Police Armed Forces 'Pietro Caruso' Legion .... pag. 45

    Special Inspectorate of Anti-Partisan Police (I.S.P.A.) .... pag. 47

    Autonomous Mobile Legion 'Ettore Muti' .... pag. 50

    Special Autonomous Departments .... pag. 51

    Special Police Services .... pag. 57

    Special Inspectorate .... pag. 58

Activities on behalf of Jews and political persecuted people .... pag. 73

Uniforms .... pag. 83

Bibliography .... pag. 97

INTRODUCTION

Even the Social Republic had its own Public Security structure, the Republican Police Corps, formed by a sort of double soul, a territorial one, engaged in the institutional tasks of the Police, and one more distinctly derived from the terrible period that was being experienced, devoted mainly to the persecution of the political opponents of Fascism, the partisans, and to hunting the Jews. At times these two souls interpenetrated, although the division remained very clear. Up to now, very little has been written about the events of the Republican Police, research has concentrated, for different and sometimes opposing reasons, mainly on those para-police units, often known as 'gangs', dedicated to the most violent and cruel activities, which mostly operated in close dependence with the Germanic commands. Instead, the more institutional aspect of the Republican police has been left out, in whose ranks many honest and probable men militated, who, in many cases, also worked to save Jews or secretly served in the Resistance. Far from producing a systematic and exhaustive study, an attempt has been made in these pages to summarise all the aspects characterising the structure of the police during the period of the Italian Social Republic.

The author

▲ The tragic Armistice of 8 September 1943 also tragically overwhelmed the Regia Polizia. On 12 September, on the Piazza del Viminale, the SS officers and Carabinieri guarding the Ministry of the Interior were disarmed by German paratroopers.

▲ Carabinieri and police, after being disarmed and placed in ranks, are waiting to know their fate.

▼ Police officers are sent to concentration and imprisonment points, under the control of the German paratroopers, who have occupied the capital.

THE REPUBLICAN POLICE

The fall of Fascism also suddenly affected the Public Security organs: in the Police Headquarters, orders from the higher authorities and a clear stance from the Sovereign were awaited in vain, which were not forthcoming. Badoglio proceeded to establish a court martial and to remilitarise the Public Security Corps[1], to the lapels of whose jackets the fasces lictori were to be removed and the stars affixed. Between 25 July 1943 and 8 September, therefore, the Police went through a period of limbo, during which the agents were aware of an irreparable rupture in the balance of government, a situation that was not easy to decode, made even more uncertain by the absence of clear orders; certainly the activity against anti-fascists was reduced, even though Badoglio feared the activity of the socialist and communist movements. The custody of Mussolini at Campo Imperatore was entrusted to a nucleus of police officers, commanded by Questore Gueli (who later joined the Social Republic), equipped with automatic weapons and machine guns, who did not, however, react against the German paratroopers who, on 12 September, with Operation Oak, freed the Duce from captivity.

With the Armistice, the situation precipitated abruptly: the policemen were consigned to barracks and police headquarters, fearing retaliation by the Nazis. Following the Armistice of 8 September 1943 and the German occupation of the capital, the German authorities arrested Police Chief Carmine Senise[2] on 23 September, accused of having participated in the coup against Benito Mussolini and therefore considered an untrustworthy character. Senise was captured by German SS soldiers and paratroopers, under the command of Captain Erich Priebke, while in his office at the Viminale. After the fall of Fascism, in fact, Senise had been appointed Chief of Police by Badoglio, as he was closer to the Monarchy than to the Regime.

Meanwhile, the Duce, following the establishment of the Italian Social Republic, gave impetus to the creation of new administrative and military apparatuses, including the simultaneous organisation of the Republican Police and the Republican National Guard. Mussolini realised that the management of public order could absolutely not be entrusted to the Carabinieri Corps, which had proved to be a potential danger due to its loyalty to the House of Savoy. In October 1944, the central police apparatus was transferred to northern Italy. According to the testimony of some officers, one night in October the order came to load all available vehicles with equipment and supplies: printing presses, uniforms, weapons, dossiers, equipment of all kinds were crammed into any vehicle and a long column quickly set off at night from Rome towards northern Italy. Once they reached Valdagno (VI), all the material was placed in some warehouses of a wool mill, temporarily used as a ministerial facility.

---

1 The Corps of Public Security Officers was a purely civil corps and during World War II had only mobilised a couple of motorised battalions, equipped with motorbikes, in Montenegro and the Rijeka area.

2 Born in Naples in 1883, Senise graduated in Law in 1908, won a competitive examination and entered the Ministry of the Interior, where he held positions as Subprefect, Secretary and then Head of the Press Office, to be subsequently assigned to the General Directorate of Prisons and then to the Directorate of Health. In 1930 he was transferred to the General Directorate of Public Security and became Head of the Division for General and Reserved Affairs. In 1932 he was promoted to Prefect and appointed Deputy Chief of Police, taking over command on 22 November 1940 from Bocchini, at the suggestion of Undersecretary of State for the Interior Buffarini Guidi. On 14 April 1943 he was dismissed by Mussolini, who was unhappy with the weak repression of the workers' strikes in northern Italy in the previous month. Senise took part in the 25 July 'conspiracy', proposing to execute Mussolini's arrest at the Villa Savoia. On 26 July, Pietro Badoglio reinstated him in his duties, which he kept until the Cassibile armistice was announced, when he chose to remain in Rome. On 23 September, he was arrested by the Germans, deported to Germany and imprisoned first in the Dachau concentration camp and then in the Hirschegg concentration camp, where he was released on 2 May 1945. Back in Italy, he was accused of aiding and abetting Fascism, but was acquitted by the Special Court of Assizes in Rome. He died in 1958.

The Republican Police Corps was thus officially established on 20 November 1943, as part of the Armed Forces, operating in the territory of the Italian Social Republic, to perform the tasks of:

- forensic police
- public safety
- crime prevention and repression
- verification of the application of state laws
- public order
- anti-guerrilla warfare
- patrolling the peripheral territory.

This latter activity was mainly carried out by the mobile units and the so-called Armed Police Forces. The Republican Police was also in charge of the information and investigation service in relation to the country's state of war, with the application of the laws in force in this area.

In addition to the departments that formed the backbone of the Republican Police, there were also a number of units that could be defined as para-police, which were not concerned with guaranteeing legality in the strict sense of the word, but which operated in a repressive manner (often fiercely and violently) against the Resistance.

The Republican Police Corps absorbed the civil servants of the Ministry of the Interior's Department of Public Security and the members of the dissolved Regio Corpo degli Agenti di Pubblica Sicurezza (Royal Corps of Public Security Agents)[3], resulting, in fact, in a civil-law force, but with a military-style organisational structure.

The Corps took on the name of Polizia Repubblicana della R.S.I. (Republican Police Force of the Italian Socialist Republic) and was placed under the command of Prefect Tullio Tamburini[4], with headquarters in Toscolano Maderno (BS), at the Ministry of the Interior, under the authority of the Minister Regent of the Ministry. In terms of personnel, in October 1944, the Republican Police Force numbered 21,259 men, a number that was to dwindle due to wartime events down to approximately 20,000, located mainly in provincial capitals, initially organised in 10 Regional Inspectorates, 65 Police Headquarters, 2 Specialisation Schools, Escort Units detached to the various Ministries and mobile anti-guerrilla operative units[5].

---

3 The organisation of the Republican Police partly anticipated the State Police founded in 1981, as it became, by necessity, a single, unified body, unlike the system in force in the Kingdom of the South, where the police continued to consist of the civil servants of the Ministry of the Interior and the Royal Corps of Public Security Agents.

4 Born on 22 April 1892 in Prato, he moved to Florence before the Great War, where he lived by his wits; convicted of fraud and forgery of banknotes, he avoided prison as a 'confidant with the Police headquarter'. After fighting, at the end of the conflict he enrolled in the Florentine Fascio, making a rapid rise in the ranks, taking part in numerous punitive expeditions in the early 1920s, but always managing to avoid convictions and imprisonment, while continuing his illicit activity as a swindler. In 1923, he was appointed consul of the 92nd Militia Legion 'Francesco Ferrucci', which he commanded at his own discretion, sometimes employing his subordinates to protect his personal interests. On the night between 3 and 4 October 1925, he unleashed anti-Masonic violence in Florence, being accused from various quarters of bringing Fascism into disrepute with his violent deeds, so much so that he was expelled from Italy and sent to Libya. Returning to Italy in 1936, he was appointed Prefect of Avellino in 1936 and of Ancona in 1939, and finally of Trieste from 7 June 1941 to 1 August 1943. After the Armistice, on 12 September, he again took up the post of Prefect of Trieste, which he held until 1 October, when he was appointed Head of the Republic Police Corps. Tamburini did not abandon his old criminal methods and in January 1944 he was accused of unlawful enrichment and was dismissed in April. Suspected of connivance with the Allies, General Karl Wolff had him arrested in Como on 21 February 1945 and subsequently interned in Block 25 of the Dachau concentration camp. At the end of April, together with other distinguished prisoners, he was transferred to Villabassa in Val Pusteria, where he was released by the Allies on 4 May 1945. However, he was soon arrested for his involvement with the Regime and was nevertheless amnestied in September 1946. He emigrated to Buenos Aires, returning to Rome years later, where he died in 1957.

5 Naturally, the number of personnel thinned out as the territory of the Social Republic came under Anglo-American control, just as the Police headquarters and Regional Inspectorates were gradually reduced.

The formation of the Republican Police was not, however, a mechanism for the (re)foundation of the Corps, but relied, at least as far as the territorial structure was concerned, on the already existing bodies of the Corps of Public Security Agents, since the Police Headquarters had continued to carry out their institute functions without interruption even during the delicate moments following the Armistice. For this reason, the adhesion to the Social Republic was, for many policemen, not a conscious adhesion, but rather the mere execution of an order. It was probably not even clear to many what the R.S.I. was and what military service in the Republican Police meant. The situation only became clear to everyone when, with the formal and symbolic act of removing the stars from their lapels and replacing them with Republican gladiators, they were hastily asked to swear allegiance to Mussolini: on hearing the news of this change of sides, many policemen who had sworn allegiance to the King did not hesitate to desert, going into hiding or joining the ranks of the Resistance. It is necessary, however, to emphasise how the events that the Republican Police underwent after its constitution were tormented by the magmatic situation in which the territory of the Social Republic found itself, a situation that led to ever-increasing tensions as the civil war worsened, in the knowledge that the situation was very different from province to province and that both the way of policing and the system of partisan fighting changed. The Republican Police found itself in an uncomfortable position: frowned upon by the fascists, because it was considered a structure where ambushers lurked, and equally frowned upon by the Resistance, because the partisans considered it a fascist organisation, so much so that for many, life in the Republican Police was always a perennial race for survival.

The reality experienced at that time was so intricate that there were also many cases of policemen who were known and respected by the partisans, because they were considered to be professionally honest men who were not involved in anti-Partisan persecution, and who were therefore always spared from Gappist attacks and episodes of retaliation. These men were also respected when, having received a proposal to desert to join the Resistance, they refused in the name of the oath of loyalty they had taken.

Among the Republican Police force there were, however, as a result of the extremely confused state of affairs, a certain number of desertions, men who decided to join Resistance formations, very often urged on precisely by the upsurge in anti-Partisan fighting, perpetrated above all by the 'Special Police Units'. Numerous were the members of the Police who perished taking up arms as partisans. Auxiliary guard Flavio Grandoni of the Turin Police Headquarters, after deserting from his Battalion, had joined the partisan formations of the 'Garibaldi' Brigade. He died near the capital of Piedmont during a firefight against Nazi formations fighting as a partisan on 26 August 1944.

Not all the escapees, however, were welcomed with open arms by the partisans. On 15 June 1944, for example, fourteen very young auxiliary officers of the Modena Company[6] attempted to join the partisans of the so-called Republic of Montefiorino. The Modenese National Liberation Committee provided the policemen with a letter guaranteeing their democratic faith and their desire to join the partisans, but when the agents reached the area in the hands of the partisans, they were captured by a formation led by a ruthless commander, Nello Pini, battle name 'Nello', who decided to shoot them immediately under the false accusation of being spies[7].

---

6 The fourteen young men were Officers Emilio Campeggi, Giuseppe Casari, Aderigo Cassanelli, Alessandro Castellari, Raffaele Del Bue, Angelo Giubbolini, Guerrino Gozzi, Nando Montorri, Silvio Moscardini, Luigi Piana, Riccardo Quadrelli, Tullio Tripoli, Livio Varagnoli and Enrico Visciano.

7 Although commander 'Nello' was a valiant fighter, he was soon judged ruthless and uncontrollable by the Montefiorino Resistance command for this massacre and for the systematic and unjustified elimination of other prisoners. Nello Pini was arrested and on 31 July 1944 was shot in Montefiorino by the same partisans, together with some members of the General Staff of his unit.

Several police elements acted as a 'fifth column' within the same police headquarters, often paying with their lives for their support to the Resistance, after being discovered. In La Spezia, the German authorities intercepted a nucleus that acted from inside the local Questura (Police Headquarters), thanks also to confessions extracted from some agents by torture, and all those identified were deported and almost all perished in captivity. In Bologna, in the early morning hours of 21 July 1994, the auxiliary Guards Romeo Giori and Paride Pasquali together with another partisan were shot in Piazza del Nettuno. The two auxiliary Guards were on duty at the Strada Maggiore Police Station in Bologna and were secretly members of the Resistance, but were discovered and arrested. Transferred together with a third partisan to the command of the Compagnia Ausiliaria in Bologna, they were viciously tortured by the infamous 'Tartarotti gang' (the Special Autonomous Company of the Auxiliary Police), which we will discuss later.

On the other hand, there was no lack of episodes of violence and ferocity perpetrated by elements of the police who, taking advantage of the lacklustre situation in northern Italy, deviated from the duties of public security and dedicated themselves to violent repressive actions, which in some cases resulted in expressions of outright banditry. These methods led to an intensification of partisan attacks, especially against the agents and officers of the political squads; unfortunately, there were also episodes of operations carried out against elements completely unrelated to the repressive activity; we can cite the case of the bomb attack against the barracks of the Police Officers' Company in Bologna on 1 November 1944, which caused 7 deaths, including officers and non-commissioned officers.

In other cases, elements of the Republican Police found themselves involved in firefights with partisans, while they were deployed in actual anti-rebel operations. On 3 March 1944, for example, partisans of the Gramsci Brigade attacked and occupied the barracks of the Republican National Guard in Poggio Bustone (RI) and repelled a counter-offensive led by 200 police officers, Republican National Guard militiamen and Army soldiers, commanded by the Questore (police commissioner) of Rieti, Bruno Pannaria. The latter returned to the area on 10 March, leading a new offensive, which cost the lives of three partisans and wounded five others, but a group of just 24 partisans counter-attacked in turn near Poggio Bustone, killing 10 people (according to some studies, 14 were among the Social Republic units killed), destroying many vehicles and losing four men in the fight. Among the Republican casualties at Poggio Bustone were the Quaestor of Rieti himself, Bruno Pannaria, and Public Security guards Sante Berton, Nicola Dell'Aquila, Umberto Ferretti and Gustavo Trotta. Two other officers, Alberto Guadagnoli and Vincenzo Francescucci, captured after the attack together with two G.N.R. soldiers, were shot by partisans near the ruins of the castle of Leonessa (RI)[8].

At other times, police officers lost their lives while carrying out their duties, falling victim to partisan attacks or ambushes. On 1 March 1944, two police non-commissioned officers from the Genoa Police Headquarters, Marshal Pietro Lanzi and Brigadier Amedeo Garribba, dressed in plain clothes, were tasked with providing an escort for a S.E.P.R.A.L. truck (the government agency that was in charge of food distribution and supply during the war). In the early hours of the morning, on the road between the villages of Sarmato and Rottofreno (PC), the truck they were travelling on was blocked by some partisans, who searched the cab of the vehicle and found Marshal Lanzi's service pistol. The partisans asked who the gun belonged to, and Marshal Lanzi was forced to reveal his identity. The two non-commissioned officers were then captured and forced to follow the partisans, probably in order to serve as objects in a possible prisoner exchange with the R.S.I. authorities; two weeks after the capture, on 14 March, Brigadier Garribba was shot and about a week later, on the

---

[8] Their bodies were not found and the two policemen were officially declared missing. It was not until 2004 that human remains were found in the ruins of the Leonessa castle, attributable to those shot in 1944.

23rd, it was Marshal Lanzi's turn. It was only on 7 March 1946 that Marshal Lanzi's body and that of Vice-Brigadier Garribba were found in the locality of Bertassi di Ottone (PC); later, the Brigadier's body was buried in the cemetery of Gorreto (GE). The case of Police Guard Giovanni Polistri, who died in Via Cantarena in Genoa on 4 March 1944, while on patrol with other colleagues, is similar. A 'gappista', realising the presence of the agents, suddenly opened fire on the group: Polistri died instantly while another agent, Giordano Melchiorre, was wounded in the hand.

Another example. On the afternoon of 2 July 1944, in Sestri Ponente, deputy brigadier Mario Devoti, on duty at the town's police station after having served in the Genoa Mobile Squad, was murdered by a partisan. Around 3 p.m., the policeman was fatally shot by an individual who had come up behind him while walking along Piazza Aprosio. The murderer was an 18-year-old from Cuneo, Bruno Raspino, who was caught almost immediately, having been found in possession of the gun with which the policeman had been killed. The young man, when cornered, confessed to the murder, was tried, sentenced to death and put to death shortly afterwards.

Even with regard to the Jewish residents in Italy, the Republican Police was to operate in concert with the German authorities, according to the orders issued by the Head of the Corps. On the evening of 30 November 1943, in fact, Tamburini sent the following police order to the Prefectures, which he signed:

"*Notice is hereby given, for immediate execution, of the following police order to be enforced throughout the territory of this province*:

1. *All Jews, even if discriminated against, to whatever nationality they belong, and in any case resident in the national territory must be sent to special concentration camps. All their movable and immovable property is to be immediately seized pending confiscation in the interests of the Italian Social Republic, which will use it for the benefit of the destitute victims of enemy air raids.*
2. *All those who, born of mixed marriages, were recognised as belonging to the Aryan race in application of the racial laws in force, must be subject to special vigilance by the police organs.*
3. *Let the Jews therefore be concentrated in provincial concentration camps, waiting to be gathered in specially equipped concentration camps'.*

In fact, as of the following 1 December, this ordinance made every Jew liable to arrest by the Italian authorities, and caused new concentration camps to be set up in Italy, thus creating the basis for ensuring the dispatch and subsequent annihilation of Italian Jews to extermination camps. The order required prompt and prompt execution by the police organs, in particular the Political Offices of the Police Headquarters.

As far as 'deviated' police elements are concerned, let us mention, by way of example, the case of the so-called 'Polga gang', which acted in the province of Vicenza and was made up of elements from the capital's police headquarters. On 21 November 1943 in Vallonara di Marostica (VI), some partisans killed Alfonso Caneva in an ambush: he was the first republican from Vicenza to be executed. The fascists' response was immediate and 14 people were arrested in Marostica, who suffered savage mistreatment. Among the Republican units engaged in the repressive action was the Vicenza Auxiliary Police Battalion, commanded by Captain Giovanni Battista Polga. From that moment on, Captain Polga began to make himself infamous for his crudeness and efficiency in repressing anti-fascists, directing many round-up actions against partisan formations in Vicenza and being responsible for various executions, including of civilians. Polga, who had forged close relations with the Nazi BdS-SD, also formed a 'gang', which passed itself off as a partisan formation, committing looting and violence throughout the province. On 27 November 1944, an 'anti-Polga' action group, made up of elements close to the Resistance, after having infiltrated the ranks of the Questura for some time, discovered the Captain's plan for the following day and organised an ambush together with some partisan formations, in order to execute the death sentence imposed by the Provincial C.L.N. on Polga himself. The next day, at around 10 a.m., a team of partisans carried out the ambush near Priabona di Monte di Malo (VI), executing the death sentence. This partisan action caused a great stir throughout the province and the revenge was rabid. From the following day, and until the beginning of December, the province of Vicenza was combed and numerous partisans were killed, even by elements of the Vicenza Auxiliary Republican Police Battalion, while the ferocious Captain Polga was celebrated as a martyr to the Republican cause. In the Vicenza Police Headquarters itself, on the other hand, several agents of the Auxiliary Police became employees of the German Police and were employed as informers. Among them was a certain Dal Zotto Anselmo, one of the few, against whom documented accusations emerged for having actively worked to have some partisans from Schio sent to German concentration camps.

Another violent and ferocious unit was present at the Republican Police Headquarters in Novara: it was the so-called 'Squadraccia', a para-police unit under the command of Public Security Lieutenant Vincenzo Martino. The Special Squad, nicknamed the 'Squad' precisely because of the methods adopted, became notorious for the brutality with which it persecuted elements considered to be political antagonists of Fascism, without even sparing members of the Republican Police itself, such as, for example, Deputy Auxiliary Brigadier Pasquale Squadrito, who was summarily killed on 21 June in Novara by elements of the 'Squad', because he was connected with the Resistance in the Novara area, for which he was doing his best to recruit partisans. On 1 November of the same year, Lieutenant Martino's unit also murdered Brigadier Giovanni Barberi of the Novara Police Headquarters Auxiliary Battalion. Brigadier Barberi had been identified by Martino's Special Unit thanks to the confession of another partisan, who, during a brutal interrogation, had admitted that the Brigadier supplied the partisans with weapons, ammunition and clothing, which were regularly taken from the Questura warehouse with the help of other soldiers from the Auxiliary Police Battalion. After being arrested, Barbari was taken to one of the hiding places of the stolen material, but the car carrying it had a breakdown; taking advantage of the moment of confusion, the Brigadier attempted to escape, but was shot by machine-gun fire.

Lieutenant Martino, arrested immediately after the war for the execution of Squadrito and accused of numerous other crimes, managed to escape from captivity, never to be captured again.

25 April 1945 marked the political end of the Italian Social Republic and, consequently, also that of the Republican Police. At the time of the partisan insurrection, General Renzo Montagna did not handle the transition of power, both military and political, as would be the task of a Chief of Police, even at personal risk, to protect public order, but stayed, together with Minister Pisenti and Chief of Province Bassi, at Palazzo Monforte in Milan until 4.00 a.m. on 26 April without issuing orders. This attitude can be explained by the fact that, already since mid-April 1945, with Mussolini's authorisation, Montagna had been maintaining contacts with figures from the Milanese C.L.N.[9]. Having gone into hiding, he was, however, later identified and was amnestied by the Special Court of Assizes in Como on 29 May 1947. In fact, the partisan Nino Puleio, commander of the 10th Division of the Matteotti Brigades, in an article in the socialist daily 'Avanti!'[10], declared that between January and April 1945, some socialist partisans had managed to carry out important proselytising work within the Milan Police Headquarters and the barracks located in the city, so much so that the Matteotti Brigade Command planned to set up a special Brigade in Arona (NO), made up of police

---

9 For this reason, Renzo Montagna was accused of double-dealing in anonymous letters sent to the periodical 'Asso di Bastoni' after the war.
10 'That April in Milan', cited in bibliography.

officers and officials who had expressed a willingness to side with the Resistance, which would be placed under the command of Puleio himself. These elements were to abandon the units in case the Allied advance became difficult, they were to move to Arona with their weapons and from there they were to start operating in concert with the other partisan formations; however, in mid-April 1945, the Republican secret services discovered the plot and arrested him, on his way back from a meeting with two Milan police officers, Pigola and Parascandolo. Taken to the Police Headquarters and brought into the presence of General Renzo Montagna, Nino Puleio is said to have shown the Chief of Police how most of the men in the Milanese police force and General Montagna, after making arrangements with his superiors, would make agreements with Puleio so that the partisan commander would undertake to manage public order in the days of the partisan insurrection, which was by then imminent (in fact, Puleio's Division was the protagonist in managing the situation in the Lombard capital in those troubled moments).

In spite of the dramatic situation of those days, many were the garrisons of the Republican Police, especially the Public Security Police, who remained steadfast, giving continuity to their institute activities. In several cases the guards intervened to defend the citizens threatened by the fleeing German units, as happened for example in Cuneo, where five agents of the local Questura were killed during some clashes between German soldiers and citizens on 28 April 1945. These are the names of the five fallen in Cuneo:

- Guard Mario Coscia
- Guard Marco Evangelista
- Brigadier Ugo Marano
- Guard Nazzareno Pellegrini
- Guard Agostino Scarpaci

With the partisan uprising, those who had already made contact with the resistance formations or who even acted as a fifth column, infiltrated within the police structures, were also able to emerge. Many were those who paid with execution for the position they held under the Social Republic, such as, to mention some of the most striking cases, the Questore of Novara Emilio Pasqualy, the Questore of Como Lorenzo Pozzoli or the Questore of Brescia Manlio Candrilli, who was arrested at home because he thought he had always acted correctly, and hastily tried and executed. Among the corpses displayed in Piazzale Loreto together with Mussolini's was that of Captain Mario Nudi, in charge of the Duce's escort. Nudi had been shot by partisans on 28 April on the lakeside in Dongo (CO), together with other members of the so-called 'Mussolini Column'. The capture and killing of Nudi are surrounded by a veil of mystery, since according to some historians the Captain was eliminated because he was an inconvenient witness to the disappearance of the famous 'gold of Dongo': in fact, the Captain was one of those responsible for the safekeeping of the famous 'gold of Dongo' and was handed over to the armed forces after being robbed of the precious cargo. What is certain is that he was subjected to a summary trial by the partisans, a trial that lasted no longer than 10 minutes, just enough time to be sentenced to death, despite Nudi's proven extraneousness to war crimes or other similar heinous acts.

On the other hand, it is incredible how the last Republican police chief, General Renzo Montagna, managed to get through the partisan insurrection unscathed. He emerged from the trial held by the Como Extraordinary Court of Assizes without any consequences, being able to retire to a quiet private life in Voghera (PV). This paradoxical situation was probably motivated by the fact that, as we have just seen, Montagna had weaved plots with the top leadership of the National Liberation Committee in Milan during the last month of the war.

Other elements, compromised during fascism, worried about their fate, tried to disappear from circulation, taking advantage of the help offered by relatives and friends in the area.

But many were also simple officers who paid with their lives in those dramatic days, often without any real motive or involvement, often without even standing trial, guilty of having worn a uniform at such a troubled time.

At the end of the war, the Republican Police was absorbed by the newly formed Corps of Public Security Agents. Not all members of the Republican Police were allowed to remain in the ranks of the Corps: many were ousted from operational activity after being judged unfit by the partisan purge commissions.

Organigram

- General Headquarters - Valdagno (VI) then Toscolano Maderno (BS):
    - Chief of Police
    - Intendency
    - Autonomous Public Security Battalion[11]
    - Car park

The function of Chief of Police was assumed by:
    - Prefect Tullio Tamburini, from October 1943 to April 1944;
    - Prefect Eugenio Cerruti, from April 1944 to 5 October 1944[12];
    - General Renzo Montagna, 6 October 1944 to 25 April 1945[13].

- Escort Units seconded to different Ministries:
    - Presidential Team, assigned to the security of the Head of Government
    - Ministers' Escort Units
    - Undersecretary of State Escort Unit

---

11 On 23 November 1944, the Battalion suffered a terrible disaster. Three Auxiliary Guards on the force, who had gone to the village for food supplies, on their way back to the Battalion's headquarters found a shell holder containing two unexploded ordnance, the residue of an Allied raid that had taken place a few days earlier. The three policemen took steps to avoid danger to the population and, following official orders, picked up the unexploded ordnance, transported it to their command post, which was located in Villa Carcarini in Virle Treponti (a hamlet in the municipality of Rezzato, where some offices of the R.S.I. Ministry of the Interior had been detached) and deposited it at the entrance. Having alerted the garrison commander, chosen guard Valfredo Buti, the soldiers tried to defuse the devices, one of which, however, exploded. Commandant Buti, who was standing on the threshold of the command post, and Guard Giovanni Imma were torn apart by the deflagration, while the other two officers were injured, one seriously. Choice Guard Valfredo Buti died during transport to hospital, while Auxiliary Guard Giovanni Imma died in hospital on 11 December as a result of the very serious injuries he sustained in the incident.

12 Like his predecessor, he too was viewed with suspicion by the German authorities and was soon arrested for this reason.

13 Renzo Montagna was born in Santa Giulietta (PV) on 13 March 1894. After fighting in the First World War as an artillery officer, he founded the Fasci in Santa Giulietta and enlisted on 1 February 1923 in the M.V.S.N., commanding the 38th Legion in Asti, then the 3rd in Cuneo and in 1929 the IX Legion Group. He took part in the Ethiopian War with the rank of Consul General, commanding the 4th Battalion Group CC.NN., which occupied Amba Alagi on 28 February 1946. In the Second World War he served as Commander of the Ljubljana Presidium (from July 1942) and the CC.NN. Regiment '21 Aprile'. "21 April'. Arrested after the fall of Mussolini on 25 July 1943, he was imprisoned in Fort Boccea, where he was freed by German paratroopers on 12 September. With the birth of the Social Republic, he was appointed interim General Commander of the reconstituted Milizia, a post he held from 17 to 30 September, and then Tactical Commander of the M.V.S.N. Alta Italia. After taking part in the so-called 'Verona trial' (he was one of the 8 effective judges), at dawn on 9 July, while in his villa in Monteceresino (PV) recovering, Montagna was subjected to an attempted kidnapping by partisans. The attack was repelled by his order and by the general himself, who had joined the defenders. On 5 October 1944, he took over as Chief of the Republican Police, replacing the resigning Eugenio Cerruti, characterising his work by his energy and by putting the Special Police Departments under control, including the Economic Police in charge of the 'black bag'. He died in Voghera on 6 July 1978.

- Postgraduate schools[14] - Commander Colonel Larice:
  - School for Agents - Padua
  - School for Officers - Padua
- Regional Inspectorates of Public Security:
  - Piedmont
  - Lombardy
  - Liguria
  - Emilia-Romagna
  - Veneto
  - Venezia Giulia

organised out of 65 Questuras in 1943, reduced to 36 in October 1944, due to the Anglo-American advance.

- Armed Police Force
  - 6 Autonomous Republican Police Battalions
  - Police Armed Forces 'Pietro Caruso' Legion
  - Ettore Muti' Autonomous Mobile Legion
  - Special Inspectorate of Anti-Partisan Police (I.S.P.A.)
  - various Special Autonomous Departments

According to a document dated 4 December 1944, the following Divisions are also active:
- Political Police Division (based in Valdagno)
- Public Security Personnel Division (based in Valdagno)
- General and Reserved Affairs Directorate (based in Valdagno)
- Police Division (based in Valdagno)
- Armed Police Force Division (based in Milan)
- Border Police and Transport Division (based in Valdagno)
- Contract and Supply Management Division (based in Valdagno)

Armament

The armament of the Republican Police consisted of pistols of heterogeneous manufacture, Model 91 muskets (in all its declinations), Beretta MAB38 machine guns, some Breda and Fiat machine guns, and hand grenades (the armament of the Autonomous Formations is not covered).
According to a mirror from October 1944, the Republican Police had, in total, the following armament at that date:
- 24,500 guns
- 2,400 MAB machine guns
- 18,500 muskets
- 140 machine guns
- 800,000 cartridges
- 60,000 hand grenades.

---

14 From a document dated 4 December 1944 ("Istituzione Comando Presidio Forze di Polizia di Torino", photostatic copy in the author's possession) we learn that an Auxiliary Police School was in operation in Turin, which was dissolved on 1 December of the same year. Furthermore, a document dated 3 March 1945 ('Richiesta stralcio nominativi Guardia di Finanza', photostatic copy in the author's possession) shows that a Police School was also active in Varese. Finally, some texts erroneously indicate the P.A.I. (Polizia Africa Italiana) Cadet School, located in Busto Arsizio (VA), under the command of Colonel Rotondella, as dependent on the Republican Police structure. In reality, the P.A.I. was part of the Republican National Guard.

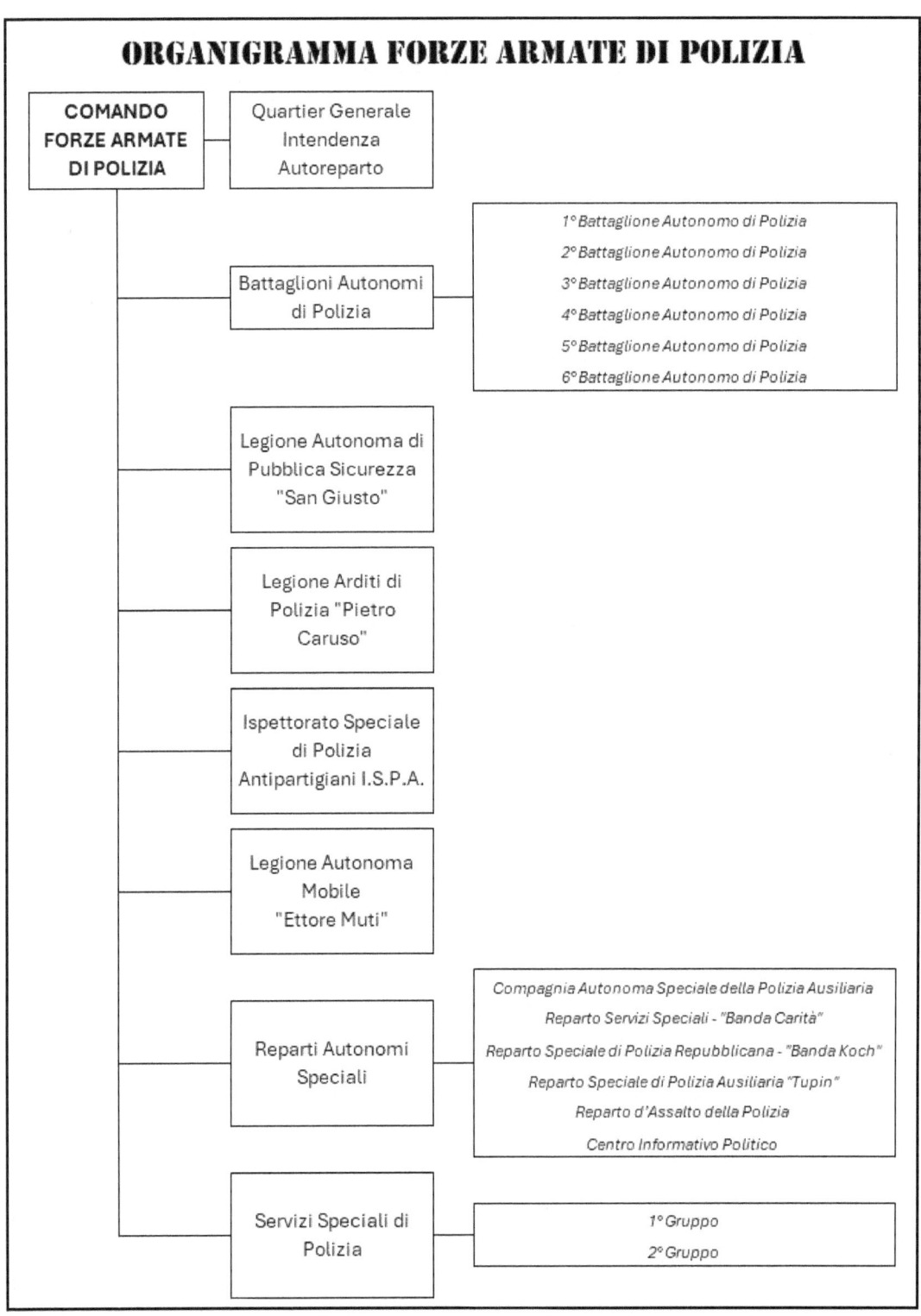

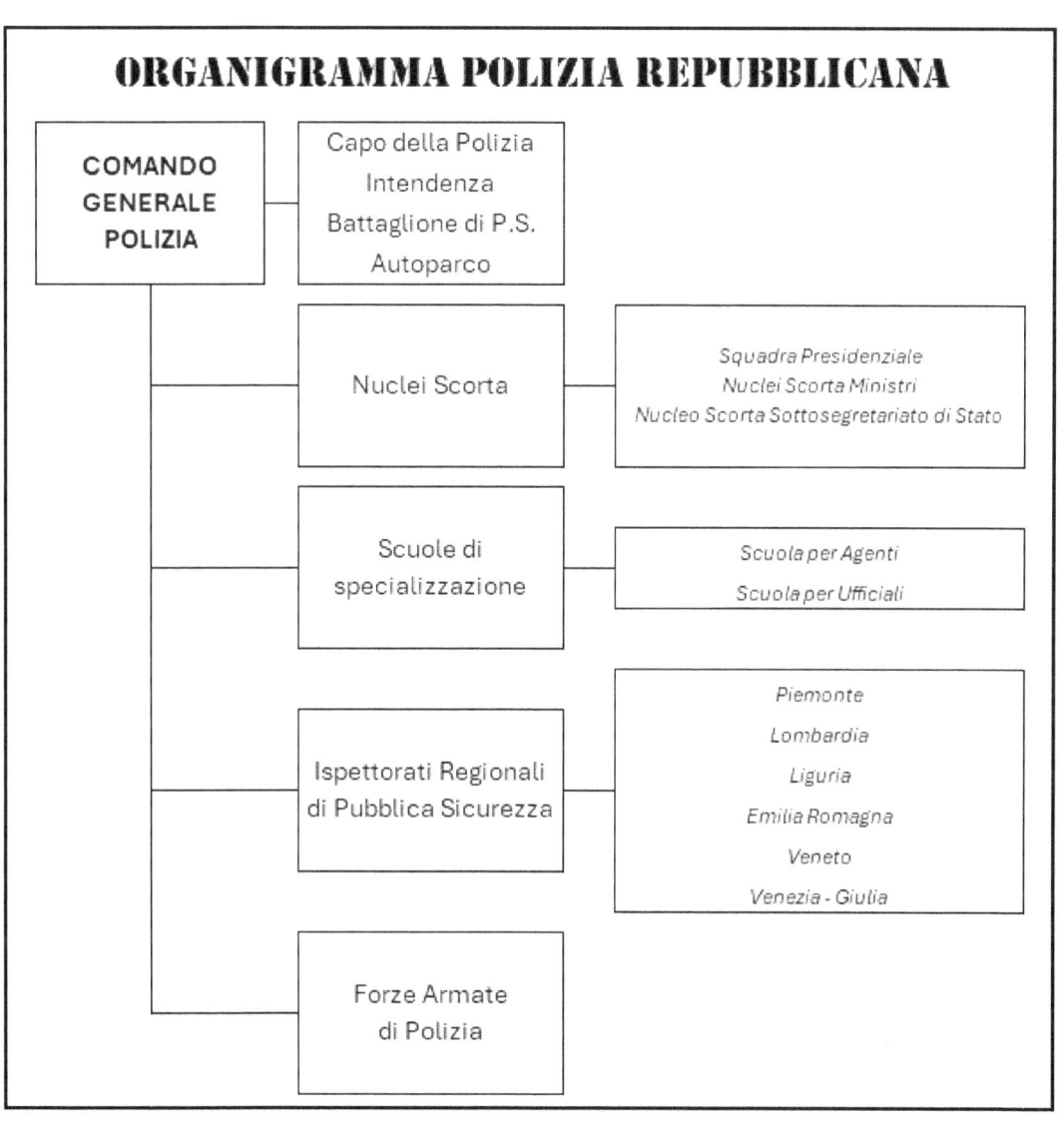

Motor vehicles

A major problem for the Republican Police was mobility. In fact, the availability of vehicles was modest, and even fuel was often lacking, as the little available was mostly requisitioned by the German Armed Forces. The vehicle fleet was therefore extremely limited and heterogeneous, based mainly on requisitioned civilian vehicles, with a few rare exceptions for the units of combat units (in particular the mobile units of the I.S.P.A.).

Armoured vehicles

The Republican Police apparatus, unfortunately, had no organic armoured units: in the context of the Italian Social Republic, the Army itself had difficulty in setting up armoured units and, as a result, the Police could only line up a few regimented vehicles.

From a document of the Regional Inspectorate for Piedmont of the Republican National Guard dated 14 March 1944, we learn that the Turin Prefecture had an armoured car of an unspecified type. In the document, which called for a combing operation along the Rivoli-Avigliana and Piossasco-Cumiana routes, an area considered to be infested by partisans defined as very active, it was in fact requested that the Prefecture of Piedmont's capital provide its own armoured car.

The Police Instruction Battalion, stationed in Turin, had an unidentified SPA chassis-mounted armoured car of an unidentified type, probably a salvage construction similar to the Black Brigade's 'Ather Capelli' armoured car. This vehicle was used in June 1944 to guard the powder magazine in Riovalmaggiore (TO). Unfortunately, no pictures of the vehicle are known and it is therefore impossible to reconstruct its colouring. Only the number plate is known: 'POLIZIA 006'.

According to Piero Berta's research, the armoured car was lost on 12 June 1944. The commander of the garrison of the Rio Valmaggiore powder magazine, a lieutenant, would have been used to go to the nearby village of Front Canavese every morning to have a coffee in peace, accompanied by some militiamen, travelling in his armoured car, which, according to the author's description, was equipped with a revolving turret, armed with a machine gun. Partisan Piero Piero (born Piero Urati), commander of the local 'Matteotti' Flying Brigade, decided to take the Republican militia by surprise and on 12 June, he ambushed them on their way back, placing a lorry sideways on the road leading to the powder magazine and hiding a dozen or so partisans in the brushwood on the hill opposite the roadblock. The police squad came under enemy attack: the soldiers marching on foot behind the armoured car were taken by surprise, were unable to react and some of them died under partisan fire. Instead, the crew of the armoured car attempted to force the blockade. Partisan Giorgio Davito jumped onto the turret of the armoured car and threatened the occupants with a hand grenade, forcing the crew to stop the vehicle; the partisan commander Piero Piero, after getting the men out of the armoured car, ordered the Republican officer to surrender, threatening to kill him and all his men. The Lieutenant then ordered his men to surrender and also allowed them to enlist in the 'Matteotti' Brigade, but only one of the republican soldiers would have joined the partisans, while all the others preferred to surrender and return home, as commandant Piero had granted them. According to this reconstruction, the entire garrison of the powder magazine would have surrendered, handing over their weapons to the partisans, who thus plundered weapons, ammunition and hand grenades. The armoured car, deprived of ammunition, was allegedly thrown into a slope; the Auxiliary Guard Carmine Scognamiglio died during the firefight[15].

---

15 According to other sources, the garrison surrendered around 8 p.m. the same day. That day, some soldiers from the Police Instruction Battalion were sent to Riovalmaggiore to guard the powder magazine, which had been left unattended following a partisan attack. Left without water, towards evening, the soldiers would organise a patrol to get water in the village. The patrol would be attacked as it was returning to the powder magazine and during the ensuing firefight many officers would be wounded, before surrendering.

The Questura di Roma had already set up a Mobile Public Security Battalion in 1938, which was based at the Fort Tiburtino barracks. The Battalion, which also included some tank drivers from the 4th Regiment, had an Armoured Company equipped with L3 tanks and AB41 armoured cars after the department was disbanded following the clashes of September 1943. The unit was employed for public order duties in the capital. When the Allies arrived, the Italian Africa Police units in Rome disbanded in an orderly manner, handing over their vehicles to the Police, including at least 11 AS42 Metropolitana trucks.

Fallen

The figure that leaps to the eye in the census of the fallen Republican Police Force is dramatic. According to studies and documentation available to date, 1,082 officers of the operational departments and 69 officials of the Public Security Administration have fallen in just 17 months of operational activity.

Many perished as a result of enemy aerial bombardment and machine-gunning: often the officers died because they were caught in the bombardment while on patrol or while they were doing their best to help the population affected by attacks from the air. Many were victims of episodes of violence and summary justice, carried out by both the partisans[16] and the Germans, who were supposed to be 'allies', but who often did not recognise the role and authority of the Republican Police[17]. On 6 June 1944, guard Vittorio Olivieri found an abandoned German army motorbike. While on his way to Terni on board the motorbike, with the intention of returning it to the German military, he was stopped by a German patrol; despite having shown his identification papers, he was believed to be a rebel and shot on the spot. A few days later, on 11 June, in Canale Nuovo di Orvieto, two German soldiers attacked and killed Agent Adami Pietro, who was on duty at the Terni Police Headquarters, to rob him of the money he was carrying. Many agents were put to the sword in the course of reprisals carried out by the Nazis, while others were captured during German army raids and deported to concentration camps because they were suspected of being part of partisan formations, without ever returning.

Not least, it must be borne in mind that most of the officers on duty lived in their private homes and that they travelled the same route to their place of duty every day, exposing them to easy ambushes by the G.A.P., especially near their homes.

Some of the fallen police officers, not belonging to the Special Forces, paid with their lives for the help they gave to Jews and political persecuted people: Yad Vashem in Jerusalem has recognised over the years several policemen deserving the title 'Righteous Among the Nations'.

Along the eastern border, once again, alongside the policemen who fell in the course of their duties, the list of the fallen grows with the names of many officers whose lives were cut short by the partisan hand, already in the days immediately following the Armistice. One example above all: Public Security guard Olivieri Antonio, on duty at the Ljubljana Police Headquarters. He was declared missing on an unspecified day after 8 September 1943, but it is known that he was captured and immediately shot in reprisal by Yugoslav partisans.

Finally, many policemen were killed or infoibrated by the Titans, for having protected the population or even just for being Italian.

---

16 Leaving aside those who died in anti-partisan activities, let us cite an extreme example that applies to all: 15 very young Auxiliary Guards of the Modena Police Headquarters Company, after having deserted on 15 June 1944 to join the resistance movement, were slaughtered by the partisans themselves, despite the fact that they had a safe-conduct guaranteeing the genuineness of their choice.

17 There are well-known cases of officers being executed because they were found, while carrying out plainclothes operations, in civilian clothes and in possession of their service weapon, despite the exemptions granted to them from the provisions of the war on the absolute prohibition of carrying weapons.

▲ Police guard Fulvio Pulcinelli, who was slaughtered by the Tito partisans behind the cemetery in Split and thrown into a mass grave in September 1943, while standing firmly at his post to ensure the service of the institution.

▲ Police officers in Rome on public order duty. Note the use of the two-coloured armband with the yellow and red colours of the Capital and the inscription 'ROMA CITTÀ APERTA - POLIZIA' (NARA).

▲ Prefect Tullio Tamburini, Head of the Republican Police from October 1943 to April 1944.

▲ The frieze of the insignia designed for the Republican Police, consisting of a wreath of oak and laurel fronds and a Republican fasces.

QUESTURA REPUBBLICANA DI PADOVA

BANDO DI ARRUOLAMENTO

1.) Sono aperti i seguenti arruolamenti nel personale Ausiliario della Polizia Repubblicana:
   - Funzionari di Polizia - Gruppo A - dal grado XI.
   - Ufficiali del Corpo della Polizia sino al grado di Capitano.
   - Sottufficiali del Corpo della Polizia.
   - Guardie Scelte e Guardie del Corpo della Polizia.

2.) L'età dei concorrenti viene così stabilita:
   - per i Funzionari di Polizia dai 25 ai 40 anni.
   - per gli Ufficiali del Corpo della Polizia dai 20 ai 30 anni.
   - per i Sottufficiali del Corpo della Polizia dai 25 ai 40 anni.
   - per le Guardie Scelte e Guardie del Corpo della Polizia dai 18 ai 30 anni.

3.) Le domande su carta da bollo da L. 8.- indirizzate al Ministero dell'Interno - Direzione Generale della Polizia - dovranno essere presentate a questa Questura corredate dai seguenti documenti e da due fotografie formato tessera:
   a) certificato di nascita.
   b) certificato di buona condotta.
   c) certificato degli studi compiuti (titolo minimo: per i Funzionari iscrizione all'Università od Istituti equipollenti - per gli Ufficiali licenza di Istituti Medi Superiori - per i Sottufficiali e Guardie licenza elementare).
   d) certificato penale.
   e) certificato di sana e robusta costituzione fisica con statura non inferiore ai m. 1.65 rilasciato da un Ufficiale medico dell'Ospedale Militare.
   f) Copia dello Stato di servizio o foglio matricolare militare.
   (Saranno titoli di preferenza quelli di studio e combattentistici).

4.) **Agli assunti sarà corrisposto il trattamento economico identico a quello attualmente vigente per il personale in servizio permanente effettivo. Agli Ufficiali, sottufficiali e guardie verrà attribuito il grado corrispondente a quello rivestito nelle forze armate.**

5.) Il termine per la presentazione della domanda scadrà il 15 giugno p. v.

Padova, 5 Maggio 1944 - XXII.

IL QUESTORE
Col. Nino G. Palmeri

▲ Call for enrollment for Auxiliary Agents of the Republican Police of the Padua Police Headquarters, dated May 5, 1944.

PREFETTURA DI VICENZA

ARRUOLAMENTI
per Personale Ausiliario della Polizia Repubblicana

In conformità di disposizioni emanate dal Ministero dell'Interno - Direzione Generale di Polizia - sono aperti arruolamenti, con assunzione immediata, nel seguente personale ausiliario della Polizia Repubblicana:

    a) UFFICIALI DEL CORPO DEGLI AGENTI DI P. S.;
    b) SOTTUFFICIALI DEL CORPO DEGLI AGENTI DI P. S.;
    c) GUARDIE SCELTE E GUARDIE DEL CORPO DEGLI AGENTI DI POLIZIA REPUBBLICANA.

Il trattamento economico sarà identico a quello vigente per il Personale in servizio permanente effettivo, pari a quello delle altre Forze armate dello Stato Repubblicano.

La scelta del personale avverrà per titoli;

Saranno titoli di preferenza quelli di studio, fascisti e combattentisti.

Gli aspiranti devono avere i requisiti seguenti:

    1) Età minima di anni 18 compiuti e massima anni 45;
    2) Essere di buona condotta morale politica e immune da precedenti penali;
    3) Essere fisicamente idoneo allo speciale servizio ed avere statura non inferiore a m. 1,65;
    4) Avere conseguito la licenza di 5ª elementare.

Le domande dovranno essere redatte su carta da bollo da Lire 8.- e dirette al Ministero dell'Interno - Direzione Generale di Polizia in Roma. Esse dovranno essere presentate o trasmesse alla locale Questura per il tramite dei Commissari Prefettizi dei Comuni della Provincia, corredate dall'atto di nascita o quanto meno di altro documento da cui risulti in modo certo la data di nascita stessa, del certificato penale e dei titoli preferenziali suaccennati.

I concorrenti dovranno essere di sana e robusta costituzione fisica, esenti da malattie costituzionali o da imperfezioni fisiche che possano limitare la idoneità del concorrente al servizio incondizionato di istituto.

A tal fine saranno sottoposti a visita sanitaria.

Il servizio prestato nel Corpo della Polizia Repubblicana vale a tutti gli effetti come servizio di leva e sarà titolo preferenziale per la successiva appartenenza definitiva alla Polizia Repubblicana.

I sottufficiali ed agenti di Polizia ausiliaria potranno fruire di alloggio e vitto in caserma.

Essi saranno assoggettati ad un conveniente periodo di istruzione.

Vicenza, 2 Febbraio 1944 - XXII

IL QUESTORE
T. Col. CESARE LINARI

IL CAPO DELLA PROVINCIA
HUGO BONALI

▲ A similar call issued in this case by the Vicenza Republican Police Headquarters.

▲ A Republican Police guard portrayed in a joking attitude in a large town in northern Italy. The soldier wears a grey-green uniform perfectly in keeping with the regulations issued during the Italian Social Republic.

PUBLIC SECURITY INSPECTORATES

The institute operations of the Republican Police, which involved the management of Public Security, the protection of laws and legality, were carried out through the capillary network of control over the territory, inherited almost in its entirety from the pre-existing structure of the Royal Police.

Six Regional Inspectorates of Public Security were established:
- Piedmont Regional Inspectorate of Public Security (headquarters: Turin - commander: Dr. Federico Rendina - P.d.C. No. 841)
- Regional Inspectorate of Public Security Lombardy (headquarters: Milan - commander: Dr. Domenico Coglitore - P.d.C. No. 795)
- Regional Inspectorate of Public Security Liguria (Headquarters: Genoa - commander: Dr. Attilio Adinolfi - P.d.C. No. 773)
- Regional Inspectorate of Public Security Emilia-Romagna (headquarters: Bologna - commander: Dr. Filippo Cordara - P.d.C. No. 751)
- Regional Inspectorate of Public Security Veneto (headquarters: Venice - commander: Dr. Giovanni Tibaldi - P.d.C. No. 853)
- Regional Inspectorate of Public Security Venezia Giulia (Headquarters: Trieste - Commander: Dr. Ciro Verdiani)

The entire Public Security apparatus was then articulated, at the second level, on the Questuras, each in a provincial capital; there were initially 65 Questuras, a number that gradually decreased with the occupation (or liberation) of Italian territory by the Anglo-Americans (by way of example, in October 1944 there were 36 Questuras)[18]:

Piedmont
- Turin Police Headquarters - 2,552 men (1,324 effective, 1,115 auxiliary and 113 recalled)
- Alexandria Police Headquarters - 411 men (87 effective and 324 auxiliary)
- Aosta Police Headquarters - 205 men (50 effective and 155 auxiliary)
- Asti Police Headquarters - 519 men (49 effective and 470 auxiliary)
- Cuneo Police Headquarters - 216 men (85 effective and 131 auxiliary)
- Novara Police Headquarters - 967 men (98 effective and 869 auxiliary)
- Vercelli Police Headquarters - 322 men (56 effective, 258 auxiliary and 8 recalled)

Lombardy
- Milan Police Headquarters - 2,802 men (1,522 effective and 1,280 auxiliary)
- Bergamo Police Headquarters - 303 men (69 effective and 234 auxiliary)
- Questura di Brescia - 528 men (195 effective and 333 auxiliary)
- Questura di Como - 828 men (180 effective and 648 auxiliary)
- Cremona Police Headquarters - 193 men (50 effective, 139 auxiliary and 4 recalled)
- Mantua Police Headquarters
- Pavia Police Headquarters - 277 men (56 effective, 215 auxiliary and 6 recalled)
- Questura di Sondrio - 61 men (47 effective and 14 auxiliary)

---

18 Where known, the number of men in charge of each Questura was indicated; the data comes from a mirror with no date, but probably dating back to the autumn of 1944 and, for this reason, the numerical consistencies of the bodies active in the territory still in the hands of the Italian Social Republic are available. For the Questuras in Venezia Giulia the data refer to October 1944.

- Varese Police Headquarters - 591 men (78 effective, 507 auxiliary and 6 recalled)

Liguria
- Genoa Police Headquarters - 1,659 men (1,068 effective, 487 auxiliary and 104 recalled)
- Questura di Imperia - 386 men (189 effective, 187 auxiliary and 10 recalled)
- La Spezia Police Headquarters
- Savona Police Headquarters - 262 men (55 active, 195 auxiliary and 12 recalled)

Veneto
- Venice Police Headquarters
- Padua Police Headquarters - 641 men (130 effective, 450 auxiliary and 61 recalled)
- Rovigo Police Headquarters - 309 men (55 effective, 240 auxiliary and 15 recalled)
- Treviso Police Headquarters - 335 men (84 effective, 220 auxiliary and 31 recalled)
- Verona Police Headquarters - 578 men (210 active, 340 auxiliary and 28 recalled)
- Vicenza Police Headquarters - 380 men (110 effective, 260 auxiliary and 10 recalled)

Venezia Giulia
- Trieste Police Headquarters - 1,194 men (340 active, 810 auxiliary and 44 recalled)
- Rijeka Police Headquarters - 207 men (85 effective, 1100 auxiliary and 12 recalled)
- Gorizia Police Headquarters - 453 men (86 effective, 340 auxiliary and 27 recalled)
- Pula Police Headquarters - 250 men (110 effective, 140 auxiliary and 10 recalled)
- Udine Police Headquarters - 407 men (115 effective, 260 auxiliary and 42 recalled)
- Zadar Police Headquarters
  After the Armistice, the Ljubljana Police Headquarters was also active, but the province soon came under direct German control and the Italian institutions were de facto cancelled. The same fate befell the Police Stations of Split and Kotor.

Emilia
- Bologna Police Headquarters
- Ferrara Police Headquarters
- Forlì Police Headquarters
- Modena Police Headquarters
- Parma Police Headquarters
- Piacenza Police Headquarters
- Ravenna Police Headquarters
- Police Headquarters of Reggio Emilia

Brands
- Ancona Police Headquarters
- Police Headquarters of Ascoli Piceno
- Macerata Police Headquarters
- Pesaro Police Headquarters

Tuscany
- Florence Police Headquarters
- Apuania Police Headquarters
- Grosseto Police Headquarters

- Livorno Police Headquarters
- Questura di Lucca
- Pisa Police Headquarters
- Pistoia Police Headquarters
- Questura di Siena

Abruzzi
- L'Aquila Police Headquarters
- Chieti Police Headquarters
- Police Headquarters of Pescara
- Teramo Police Headquarters

Umbria
- Perugia Police Headquarters
- Terni Police Headquarters

Lazio
- Rome Police Headquarters
- Frosinone Police Headquarters
- Littoria Police Headquarters
- Rieti Police Headquarters
- Viterbo Police Headquarters

From this list it is clear that auxiliary personnel, i.e. conscripts, outnumbered the actual personnel: in fact, the figures show that in the autumn of 1944 there were 7,883 regulars, 12,681 auxiliaries and 695 recalled officers, making a total of 21,259 policemen. The territorial extension of the R.S.I. underwent continuous restrictions as a result of the Allied advance and, consequently, the territorial bodies of the Republican Police were also shrinking as a result of this situation. However, most of the men employed at the Police Headquarters continued their activities even after the arrival of the Anglo-Americans, allowing them to continue to provide assistance to the law, since they were men who had not been involved in the war against the partisans, unlike those who had been employed in anti-partisan repression, who tried to defect before the Allies took their position.

Each Inspectorate had an Auxiliary Police Battalion in the regional capital, while each Questura had a militarily structured unit corresponding to a Company (Compagnia di Polizia Ausiliaria): these units had to perform public order tasks. The Auxiliary Police units also took part in anti-partisan operations, such as the 'Avanti' operation in Valdossola (9 - 23 October 1944) and the reoccupation of Alba (2 November 1944), in which Turin's Auxiliary Police Battalion took part.

It is almost certain that elements of the Questuras and combat units of the Republican Police came from the dissolved Squadre d'Azione, set up by the Federations of the Republican Fascist Party at the end of 1943. Traces of this origin can be found in a circular issued by the Secretary of the same P.F.R. Alessandro Pavolini on 22 January 1944, in which he provided useful indications for the dissolution of the Action Squads, ordering their absorption into the autonomous formations of the Republican National Guard. Point 2 of the circular, sent to Provincial Chiefs, Federal Commissioners, Quaestors and Provincial Commanders of the National Republican Guard reads:

"2. [...] *those elements who are particularly suited to the tasks carried out by the Police Headquarters and who make a request may individually pass to the Republican Police. It is understood that the latter, once admitted to the Police, must be to all intents and purposes public security agents so that the operations carried out by them are in the eyes of the citizenry and anyone else police operations, regardless of the P.F.R. membership status of these agents".*

Immediately after assuming command of the Republican Police, General Montagna sent dispositions in November to all the Questuras that were intended to curb any abuse in the act of seizures or searches, in order to restore the population's confidence in the activities of the police bodies and the security of their possessions and home inviolability:

1) *House and personal searches and seizures will be carried out, in flagrante delicto, with the assistance of a judicial police officer. Therefore, either a police officer or a commissioner or deputy commissioner must be present. Only in the absence and exceptionally will these operations be carried out with the assistance of a non-commissioned officer.*
2) *In all cases of house searches or seizures, the relevant records shall be drawn up with the assistance of the persons concerned, and in their absence suitable persons shall be called to testify.*
3) *All building doormen should be instructed to keep a list with the telephone numbers of the Police Headquarters and the nearest police offices posted at their doors.*
4) *Doorkeepers shall, as soon as officers arrive on the premises to carry out police actions, immediately inform the Police Headquarters or the nearest police office of the arrival of said officers or persons qualifying as such;*
5) *Police officers and agents who have to carry out any police operation shall, before commencing it, show the persons against whom they are proceeding the documents proving their status;*
6) *Persons arrested as a result of police operations may only be deposited in judicial prisons, and the operating bodies must inform the Questore or local commissioner of the arrest and its reasons;*
7) *Violators of these provisions, which are taken in connection with the laws, shall be reported to the competent authority, subject to administrative measures in their respect.*

The Public Security structure was also subject to German control and often obliged to accept and execute orders issued by the German authorities, with no possibility of refusal, except at great cost. Many members of the Public Security structure lived the period of the Social Republic in a constant state of mind dominated by the fear of being killed in the line of duty. This danger was perceived from all directions: one could die at the hands of an exaggerated fascist (relations between the Salò regime and the Public Security Service were often polluted by an ill-concealed lack of mutual trust) or of a German soldier, either at the hands of a partisan (who identified the policeman as a representative of the hated regime), or, at the end of the war, at the hands of some 'people's court', which sent not a few officers suspected of collusion with republican fascism to the wall.

In spite of this, the Public Security continued to operate by carrying out their official duties and many policemen performed their duty with the utmost self-sacrifice.

The situation in German Operation Zones

Particularly dramatic was the situation of the Police Headquarters of the Provinces that fell under the German aegis in the Zone of Operations of the Adriatic Coast (O.Z.A.K., Operationszone Adriatisches Küstenland), i.e. Udine, Gorizia, Trieste, Pula and Fiume, in the Operations Zone of the Pre-Alps (O.Z.A.V., Operationszone Alpenvorland), i.e. Bolzano, Trento and Belluno, in the Province of Ljubljana (Provinz Laibach) and in the Provinces of Zadar, Split and Kotor. Hundreds of agents and officials also remained in service in these police headquarters, despite German resistance, who took the oath to the R.S.I., most of them with the conviction that they had to continue to defend the citizens and the rule of law, even against German interference and Titine aims in the region. The top officials did not always hold the position of command: in some police headquarters, as in Gorizia for example, the pre-arbitrary Quaestor remained in office, while in others, such as Udine, the Quaestor was appointed by the Republican authorities, probably to replace an element considered politically unreliable. In Split, Ljubljana and Kotor, instead, the police headquarters were suppressed, while in Zadar, as we shall see in a moment, the police force met a particular fate. It is worth noting what happened in Split in the days following the Armistice: the Army, after attempting to defend the city from the Tito presence, surrendered its powers to Tito's partisans, who captured most of the men in the Police Headquarters and the prison. The Carabinieri, on the other hand, remained compact and in arms, and at first took part in the resistance against the Slavs, but later formed the "Garibaldi" Battalion, which was engaged against the Black Shirts defending the Klis fortress, located inland.

The 'surviving' Questuras in these areas operated in a climate of only formal collaboration with the German authorities, which was undermined by the increasingly pressing attempts to definitively incorporate these territories into the German Reich.

Unfortunately, the tragic events of the war that struck Venezia Giulia, Istria and the Carnaro area have almost completely obliterated all documentary traces of these men's activities and, as a result, the information available is truly fragmentary and limited. In Gorizia, for example, on 1 May 1945, when the war was over, the Titini occupied the city and began a systematic rounding up of the local population, in search of elements who were opposed to Tito's regime. At the end of the 40-day occupation of the city, 665 citizens were deported to Yugoslav concentration camps, and among them were dozens and dozens of public security officers, perceived as real enemies of the regime, the embodiment of Italian state authority.

The Zadar Police Headquarters

The events of the Police Headquarters and the Mobile Police Battalion in Zadar deserve special attention. After the armistice, the officers of the Police Headquarters and the Mobile Police Battalion, approximately 300 men, decided to remain at their posts, despite the terrible situation in the Dalmatian city. The officers and officers ensured public order services throughout the autumn-winter of 1943/'44, when Zadar suffered intense Allied bombardment, which caused the deaths of thousands of civilians and extensive material damage to the city. Following these events, the leadership of the Zadar Police Headquarters and most of the subordinates left the city. A little more than twenty officers remained in Zadar, putting themselves at the disposal of Prefect Vincenzo Serrentino, doing their best to help displaced and homeless people and trying to oppose the attempts to loot the city, which were repeatedly made by the inhabitants of the neighbouring islands.

In the course of 1944, the headquarters of the Police Headquarters and the Prefecture were reorganised on the outskirts of the city and the officers, despite their small numbers, had to work tirelessly to defend the Italian character of the city, both from German oppression, the infiltration of the Ustascia (who were driven out of Zara in July 1944 only thanks to the armed intervention of the police officers), and, finally, from attacks by Yugoslav partisans.

In August 1944, elements of the Zadar Police were accused by the German authorities of supplying weapons to Yugoslav partisans and consequently placed under arrest. The officers were freed only with the urgent intervention of Prefect Serrentino, but the Germans confiscated the weapons, ammunition, vehicles and even exhibits stored at the police headquarters.

At the end of October 1944, the Germans abandoned Zadar, effectively leaving the field open to the Yugoslav partisans. When the latter entered the town, they arrested all members of the Italian state administration, including Carabinieri and police officers, who were taken, together with several dozen civilians, to the island of Ugliano to be shot. The Carabinieri were captured despite the fact that they had taken part in the organisation of the Italian Resistance and had woven collaborative plots with the Yugoslav partisans, with whom they had made an agreement to safeguard the city's security. One of the officers, Guard Luigi Nigro, managed to free himself and take one of the jailers by surprise and disarm him, a gesture that was unfortunately useless, but which allowed other police prisoners to try to save themselves by jumping into the sea. The Titine partisans fired machine-gun volleys at the fugitives and only Guard Alessandro Bertini managed to escape. Guard Bertini and Guardsman Francesco Ragaglia, who escaped after being arrested by the Germans in August for fear of being deported to Germany, are the only two known survivors from the Zara Police Headquarters.

▲ General Renzo Montagna, the last Republican police commander, photographed here before the Armistice in the uniform of the Milizia Volontaria Sicurezza Nazionale.

▲ Captain Giovanni Battista Polga, commander of the Auxiliary Police Battalion in Vicenza, who distinguished himself for his ferocity in anti-Partisan repression.

▲ Captain Polga's coffin leaves the barracks of the Comando Battaglione Agenti di Polizia Ausiliaria in Verona. Polga had been killed during an ambush on 28 November 1944, after being sentenced to death by the C.L.N., for his crude anti-partisan conduct.

▲ The picket of honour of the Vicenza Auxiliary Police during the funeral of Captain Polga on 30 November 1944. Note how the Auxiliaries wear the M33 metal helmet, while the two officers who open the procession wear the Police high uniform.

▼ Declaration of possession of a bicycle, made on 15 November 1944 at the Legnano Police Station, dependent on the Milan Police Headquarters, by Franco Pensotti, a well-known industrialist from Lombardy. At the time, it was compulsory to report the possession of bicycles to the nearest police station (Crippa).

▲ A member of the Republican Police, probably from an Auxiliary Battalion: note the red insignia with the peculiar laurel fasces and the 'parachutist' model jacket (Crippa).

▲ Exchange of prisoners between partisans and Italian-German forces during clashes in the Ossola Valley in October 1944. On the photographer's right are some Auxiliary Officers of the Republican Police.

▼ A large group of Auxiliary Officers of the Republican Police, photographed in Val d'Ossola, at the end of Operation 'Avanti' in October 1944 (Arena).

▲ Guard of the Auxiliary Police Battalion of Verona: the photograph allows us to appreciate the details of the uniform and the use of the bandolier, dating back to the period before the Armistice.

▲ Police officer Tidona Giorgio, who was shot on 8 November 1944 by Yugoslav partisans on the island of Ugliano, in the Kornati archipelago opposite Zadar, together with most of the officers belonging to the Zadar Police Headquarters.

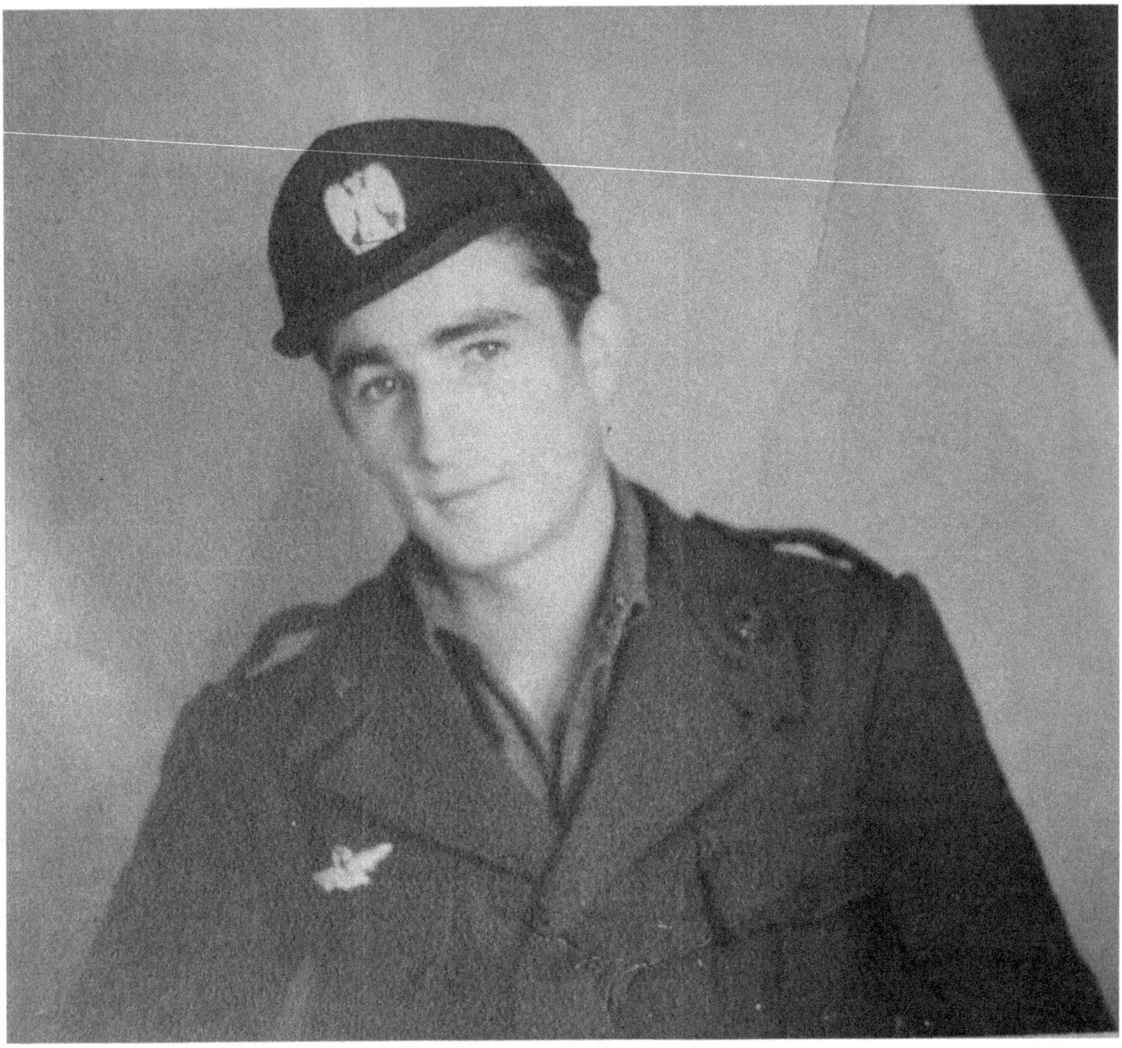

▲ Portrait of a Republican Police officer: note the cap frieze and chest badge, both embroidered in thread on cloth.

▼ Letterhead of the Bologna Police Headquarters.

POLIZIA REPUBBLICANA

QUESTURA DI BOLOGNA

Prot. N. 2191 Div. II^

Risposta a nota N. ... Addì 15 Febbraio 1945 Anno XXIII

del ... 19

Allegati N. I

OGGETTO Moggi Orlando fu Luigi- qui abitante in via Del'e Frago'e 5

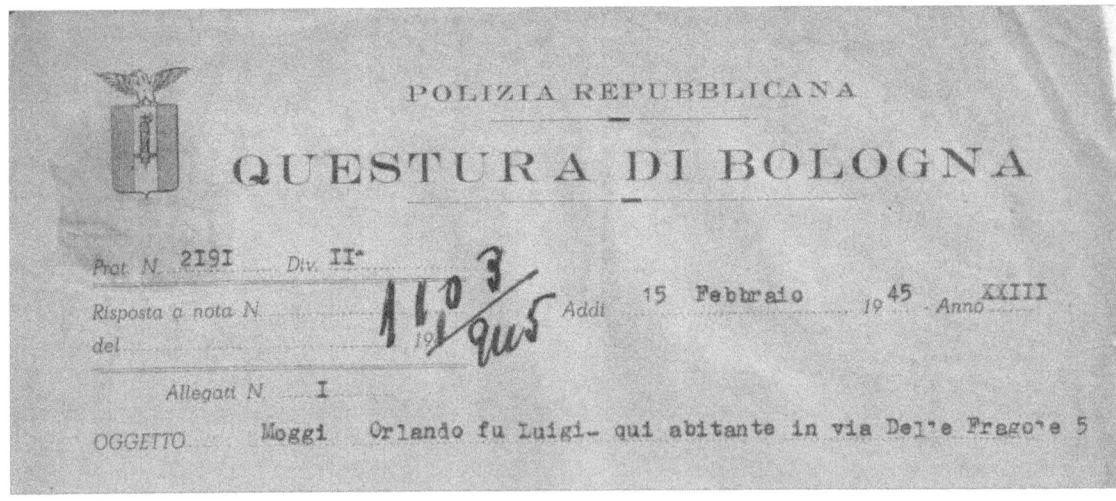

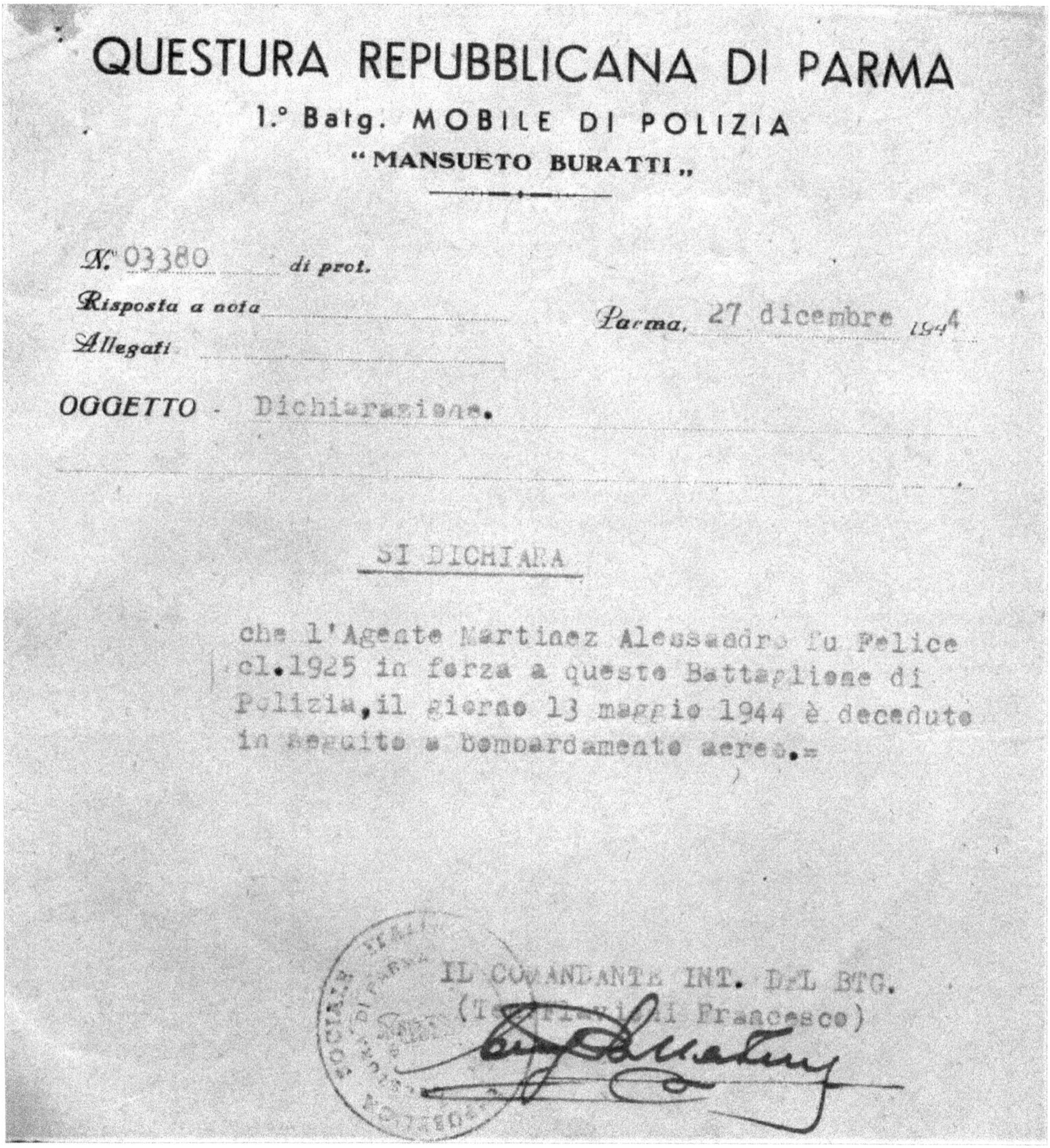

QUESTURA REPUBBLICANA DI PARMA
1.° Batg. MOBILE DI POLIZIA
"MANSUETO BURATTI"

N.° 03380 di prot.

Risposta a nota

Allegati

Parma, 27 dicembre 1944

OGGETTO - Dichiarazione.

SI DICHIARA

che l'Agente Martinez Alessandro fu Felice cl.1925 in forza a questo Battaglione di Polizia, il giorno 13 maggio 1944 è deceduto in seguito a bombardamento aereo.=

IL COMANDANTE INT. DEL BTG.
(Te.... ...i Francesco)

▲ Declaration of death of an agent of the 1st Mobile Police Battalion 'Mansueto Buratti' of the Questura di Parma, who fell during an air raid.

▲ L3 tanks of the Rome Police Mobile Battalion in the spring of 1944: note the camouflage and the police crest on the tank in the foreground. Many men and vehicles came from the 4th Carristi Regiment (Parri).

▼ Tankers from the disbanded 4th Infantry Regiment attached to the Mobile Public Security Battalion in Rome, photographed in the spring of 1944. In the centre, holding the envelope, Lieutenant Raffaello Parri, who distinguished himself in the clashes at Porta San Paolo, and who, while serving in the Police, joined the clandestine military formations of the Roman Resistance (Parri).

ARMED POLICE FORCE

In the structure of the Republican Police were grouped anti-guerrilla units, organised according to military personnel, and Special Police units under the name of Armed Police Forces, always dependent on the Ministry of the Interior.

The Armed Police Force Command was initially located in the province of Brescia, in Vobarno, but was soon transferred to the Lombard capital, Milan, and was headed by Prefect Pier Luigi Pansera, while Lieutenant Colonel Guzzardi acted as Chief of Staff.

The Command was articulated on:
- Headquarters - Commander Captain Alessandro Comoni
- Intendency - Commander Lieutenant General Italo Romegialli
- Autoreparto (in via Castelvetro 30)

all located in Milan.

A number of departments depended on the Command: 6 Autonomous Battalions, the Autonomous Legion of Public Security 'San Giusto', the Police Armed Forces Legion 'Pietro Caruso', the Special Inspectorate of Anti-Partisan Police (I.S.P.A.) and the Autonomous Mobile Legion 'Ettore Muti', as well as various Special Autonomous Units.

Autonomous Police Battalions

These Battalions were organised according to military personnel, gathering volunteers who constantly flocked to the ranks of the police. These Battalions were entrusted with the task of protecting the infrastructure, power lines and railways; the units stationed in the Po Valley were also tasked with guarding and protecting threshing operations. As a rule, the Battalions were operational at Company level, under the control of the German Commands, but in reality they had reduced strength and, in some cases, had a special position in relation to the German authorities (such as the 2nd Battalion). The Battalions were equipped with light armament, typical of the infantry: pistols, model 91 muskets, MAB 38, 8 mm Breda and FIAT machine guns, hand grenades.

In the documentation, these Battaglioni are referred to either as Battaglioni Autonomi della Polizia Repubblicana or, according to the German name, as Freiwilligen Polizei Battailon Italia (Italian Police Battalions).

1st Autonomous Police Battalion

It was stationed in Padua under the command of Lieutenant Colonel Felice Fiorentini (later transferred to command the 2nd Battalion); no further information was found.
According to some sources[19] was called 'Litorale Adriatico'.

2nd Autonomous Police Battalion

Displaced in Broni, in the province of Pavia, it was commanded by Lieutenant Colonel Alberto Guido Alfieri until 30 June 1944, then by Colonel Felice Fiorentini, until 3 March 1945, and finally by Captain Pier Alberto Pastorelli. Also known as the 'Banda Fiorentini' or 'Banda Alfieri - Fiorentini', it had a direct dependence on the German SD, which needed reliable units to be engaged in the fight against the partisans, both in armed operations and intelligence activities.

---

19 Carlo Cucut, 'The Armed Forces of the R.S.I. on the Eastern Border - September 1943 - May 1945', work cited in bibliography.

3rd Autonomous Police Battalion

It was set up in Rome in the days following the Armistice, first as a Platoon and then as a Company, being employed with military police duties around the capital, but was disbanded after its members refused to wear German uniforms.

The Battalion was (re)formed in March 1944 and was transferred to Macerata, where it supplemented some Carabinieri barracks with external garrisons. After the breakthrough of the front, the Battalion retreated to Bagnacavallo (RA) and, in June 1944, the Command, headed by Captain Giovani Gorga, was based in Castelfranco Emilia. The final structure assumed by the Battalion was:
- Command
- Command Company
- 1st Company
- 2nd Company
- 3rd Company
- 4th Company

As well as being employed to protect threshing work, on 20 August it was deployed to guard the Bologna - Verona railway line. During the winter, the battalion suffered numerous losses due to ambushes by partisan bands operating in the area, remaining in their positions until the partisan uprising in April 1945.

Other sources[20] indicate that the Battalion was initially stationed in Vercelli, only to be moved to central Italy in the Tuscan-Romagna Apennines and then north of Bologna; in the last months of the conflict it would be deployed in Friuli and absorbed by the 1st Battalion.

4th Autonomous Police Battalion

He was stationed in Treviso; no further information was found.
Other sources have him stationed in Turin.

5th Autonomous Police Battalion

The Battalion operated mainly in Gorizia and its province, with the tasks of escorting motorcars and protecting construction sites that were building defensive structures or rebuilding fortifications that had been sabotaged by the Tito partisans. The 5th Battalion was the only one to be employed in war operations, as it was deployed, above all in the Gorizia Karst (Biglia, Merna, Monte San Gabriele, Lippa di Comeno, Moncorona and from February 1945 also in Bretto di Mezzo, Jamiano, Castagnevizza and Doberdò), to defend the borders from Slavic infiltration, and for this reason suffered heavy losses: at least ninety people were killed, 37 of whom were identified, out of a total of approximately 400 men. The unit remained in arms until the end of April 1945.
Other sources give him (erroneously) stationed in Treviso.

6th Autonomous Police Battalion

It was stationed in Mestre (VE); no further information could be found.

'San Giusto' Autonomous Legion of Public Security

Department stationed in Trieste, mentioned in some publications, of which no further information is available.

---

20 Carlo Cucut, 'The Armed Forces of the R.S.I. on the Eastern Border - September 1943 - May 1945', work cited in bibliography.

Police Armed Forces 'Pietro Caruso' Legion

The Legione Arditi di Polizia 'Pietro Caruso'[21] was set up in Milan on 26 November 1944, under the Ministry of the Interior: it was a unit made up almost exclusively of very young officers, some of whom were even minors, with the exclusive task of protecting public order, with connotations very similar to those of today's Mobile Units, named after Lieutenant Colonel Pietro Caruso. In 'Il Popolo del Friuli' of Monday, 27 November 1944, there is an article that briefly describes the department's constitution ceremony:

"*General Montagna formed the 'P. Caruso' Police Armed Forces Legion.*
Milan, 27 November.

In a courtyard of the Questura, the Chief of Police General Montagna reported to the officers and agents.
After reviewing the various departments, General Montagna dictated the directives to be followed in the delicate task entrusted to the police.
The report was attended by a department with music from the Autonomous Legion 'Ettore Muti'.
Afterwards, General Montagna declared the 'Pietro Caruso' Police Armed Forces Legion constituted, whose first unit then paraded through the streets of the city, arousing great admiration for its impeccable martial behaviour'.

The Legion's commander was Lieutenant Colonel Luigi Gemma, with Lieutenant Roncisvalle as first adjutant. In a document dated 20 December 1944, it is noted that the Legion, which counted on the staff of a Company, plus services, had just been formed and was organising its headquarters in the Lombard city, under the direct command of the Chief of Police.

One of the darkest (but also mysterious) episodes in the Legion's short history was undoubtedly the execution of nine Milanese partisans on 14 January 1945 at Campo 'Mario Giurati', a sports ground that still exists in Milan. The nine young men from the Porta Romana district were accused of having joined the partisan Brigade of the Fronte della Gioventù and were condemned to death on 12 January: not all of them were eighteen years old and the oldest was 21. However, the shooting was considered a reprisal for an attack carried out in the evening at an armed forces meeting place in Via Ponte Vetero. The attack, carried out by the commander of the 3rd G.A.P. in Milan, Giovanni Pesce and the Gappist Maria Selvetti (battle name 'Lina'), had caused the death of 2 Germans and 8 Italians. The 'Caruso' was chosen by Questore Larice to supply the firing squad. According to Larice, he attended the execution, but something went wrong. After the first shot, only one of the condemned men was dead, while the other eight were unharmed or wounded, because the platoon officers had shot high and low. According to Larice, he went on a rampage, punched the Ardito Davide Dalla Chiesa with his fist, as he had clearly seen him firing in the air, and went on a terrible rant against the platoon members, accusing them of being cowards and traitors At this point Larice gave orders to Second Lieutenant Andrea Di Martino (also referred to in some sources as De Martino), the platoon commander, to fire the coup de grace at the eight condemned men who were still alive. The 24-year-old Second Lieutenant, horrified by the order he received, was brutally urged by Larice to fire 21 mercy shots: '*He had incited him to the execution with his voice and actions, pushing him and guiding his hand holding the gun*'[22] . At the end of the war, Larice was put on trial and among

---

21 Pietro Caruso was Quaestor of Rome under the German occupation, until 4 June 1944. During the Social Republic, he commanded the 3rd Portuaria Legion in Trieste until January 1944, where he also organised the seizure of gold from local Jews. After meeting Tullio Tamburini, the new Chief of Police, who appointed him Quaestor of Verona, a post he held for only a fortnight to direct public order during the 'Verona trial'. Again at Tamburini's instigation, he was assigned to the Questura in Rome. He was involved in drawing up the list of 50 names of prisoners that Herbert Kappler requested from the Italians following the Via Rasella bombing. He was sentenced to death for his involvement in the events of the Fosse Ardeatine and was executed on 22 September 1944.
22 From the records of the trial of Questore Secondo Larice.

the various charges was the execution of Campo 'Giurati'. All the members of the Campo 'Giurati' platoon were remanded for trial, as they were quickly identified a few days after the end of the war thanks to the testimony of Giuseppe Facchini. The latter, a police brigadier, was a partisan infiltrator within the 'Caruso' Legion. The Extraordinary Military War Tribunal in Milan acquitted Della Chiesa, thanks to the punch he received from Larice, while Di Martino was sentenced to death for having commanded the platoon and for firing the pardon shots, a sentence carried out on 22 May 1945 in the 'Giurati' camp[23].

Despite its short life span, the unit suffered numerous casualties. On 31 January 1944, Ardito Michele dalla Vedova disappeared from Rho (MI), and was officially declared missing as of the same date: in all probability, he was captured and killed by partisans.

On 1 February 1945, the Legion suffered its bloodiest attack, which resulted in three dead and one wounded. In the course of the night, a group of thugs attacked a roadblock in Via Gallarate, arriving on the scene in a car, and in the course of the firefight, the Arditi scelti Ettore Bianchi, Lucio Villari and Savino Corasce died, while a fourth Ardito was wounded in the arm, but survived. The assault was framed as a reprisal by the local underworld following the arrest of a person responsible for theft. The Police Headquarters phonogram of 2 February to the Provincial Chief Larice described the event in the following terms, referring to the Ardito scelto Lucio Villari: *'Wounded to death at the roadblock in Via Gallarate with Ettore Bianchi and Savino Corvasce while they were examining the documents of a stopped car. Miss Matilde Ottolina was also killed'*. On 8 February, the Ardito Ivan Pasti was killed in Via Cirene by partisans belonging to the G.A.P.; his sister Irene, only 14 years old, was also killed in the ambush.

On 13 March, Ardito Giuseppe Brusa died in Milan hospital as a result of wounds sustained in a firefight with partisans. Ardito Antonio Scapoli died on 17 April in a road accident near Sondrio, while on 21 April Ardito Pasquale Liconti died in the military hospital in Milan of an illness recognised as dependent on cause of service.

On the same day, the Ardito Antonino lo Brutto was killed near the Palace of Justice in Milan, by a partisan, who was in turn pursued by other militiamen, who executed him on the spot, after having captured him in Via Cadamosto. The story was reported in the G.N.R. bulletins as follows: *'Twenty-three-year-old Antonino Lo Brutto di Pietro, a soldier in the 'Pietro Caruso' Police Legion, was shot by an outlaw with a revolver yesterday near the Palace of Justice. The murderer, 30-year-old partisan Giulio Bianchi from Milan, was captured in Via Cadamosto and shot on the spot in accordance with the law'*. The 'Caruso' Legion also subsequently provided elements for other execution platoons for sentences carried out again at Campo 'Giurati', such as on 2 February 145, when 5 members of the Patriotic Action Groups were executed, or on 4 February, when 10 were shot.

This department lasted a relatively short time, not exceeding one year in age, and its rapid dissolution does not allow for adequate evaluation from a historical perspective. Among the structures belonging to the Republican Police, it was also the only one to be officially recognised by the Ministry of the Interior. The Legion's last casualty was Ardito Primo Armellini, who was murdered by unknown persons on 15 May 1945 in Milan's Turro district.

Some elements of the 'Caruso' Legion operated in concert with the Milanese Resistance and, for

---

23 The minutes of the trial show that Di Martino is reported to have stated: "[...] having *ascertained that the firing squad men had not fired properly on the people being shot (with the doctor), I myself fired at the partisans, discharging no less than twenty-one pistol shots, on the orders of the doctor present. The Quaestor was also present, who noted that none of the people being shot had died yet, and told me (as was the custom) to finish them off with a pistol shot. In total I unloaded three full magazines'*. Di Martino's defence was based on the assumption that he had only acted on an order he had received and that he had gone to the San Vittore prison to pick up the condemned men, unaware that they were to be shot and that they were partisans. These allegations were contradicted by the testimony of Major Gemma and the daring Renzo Torriani, who claimed that Di Martino was not only aware that he had been ordered to direct the firing squad, but was even enthusiastic about the assignment he had received.

this reason, many of them paid with their lives, such as the Ardito Giorgio Matessich, who was deported to the concentration camp in Gusen, a satellite camp of the main lager in Mauthausen (Austria), where he had been deported by the Nazis. In the course of the trial of the members of the Legion and the 'Jurors' Camp firing squad, it became clear that there was a substantial core of soldiers conniving with the Resistance within the 'Caruso' Legion. During the course of the trial, a Milanese partisan named Pachini was interrogated, who declared that a camouflaged partisan cell called 'Marat', of which he was the commander, was active within the 'Caruso' Legion. The partisan Fabris, during his testimony at the same trial, even stated that the entire Legion, considered so infamous and fascist, was actually a partisan formation in disguise[24]. Even if Fabris' assertion is certainly exaggerated, there is no doubt that there was an organised presence of partisans within the 'Caruso'. In fact, it is enough to recall that Brigadier Giuseppe Pedini received orders from Nino Puleio, commander of the 10th 'Matteotti' Division, which, as we have seen above, was to play a leading role in the dissolution of the Republican Police in Milan, and at the end of the war made as many as 157 arrests of Legion members, including commander Luigi Gemma. Lieutenant Colonel Luigi Gemma was sentenced to death by the Court of Special Assizes, but the death sentence was never carried out.

Special Inspectorate of Anti-Partisan Police (I.S.P.A.)

A body subordinate to the Political Police Division of the Ministry of the Interior, the I.S.P.A. was officially established on 1 August 1944 in Brescia, with tasks mainly related to 'intelligence' and the prevention and repression of the partisan phenomenon, although some sources date its establishment as far back as November 1943.

According to the Circular of the Ministry of the Interior, which sanctioned the establishment of the I.S.P.A., the tasks of this police body were:

a) *"[...] in urban centres. Identification, surveillance and repression of leaders and members of National Liberation Committees and Partisan Action Groups carrying out anti-national activities;*

b) *in rural centres. Identification of partisan bands, ascertainment of their location and movements, numerical strength and consistency of armament of each band.*

The Inspectorate also aims to:

1) *to sound out the political morale and the factual situation where I.S.P.A. employee sectors operate;*

2) *provide direct repressive action, through the use of Mobile Units, against G.A.P. and C.L.N. elements carrying out anti-national activities in urban centres and against their financiers and collaborators'.*

As can be seen from this programme circular, the Inspectorate was an organisation fully committed to the fight against the partisans and against political subversion towards the Social Republic and republican Fascism, organised in an articulate manner to strike and eliminate any actual or pending threat.

The Ispettorato Speciale Polizia Antipartigiana had its headquarters in Brescia (via Mantova 44) and was organised on two levels, five Sectors, assigned to investigation and prevention activities, and two Mobile Nuclei, real combat units assigned to armed operations and the repression of elements belonging to the G.A.P. and the National Liberation Committees:

---

24 According to some testimonies, when the court asked Fabris to provide some proof of what he had said, the partisan officer pulled out, in a deliberately blatant gesture, a packet of documents signed by General Raffaele Cadorna, Commander-in-Chief of the Corpo Volontari della Libertà, from a yellow bag.

- I.S.P.A. Command (Brescia)
- 5 Sectors
    - Turin Sector (based in Via Avogrado 41)
    - Milan Sector
    - Padua Sector
    - Trieste Sector
    - Brescia Sector
- 2 Mobile Assault Units
    - Nucleo Mobile d'Assalto Brescia
    - Nucleo Mobile d'Assalto Torino

Each Sector was placed under the responsibility of an Auxiliary Public Security Officer and each Sector organised a capillary network of informers, very ramified but with watertight compartments, to guarantee the greatest possible security both outside and within the organisation itself. Each Sector collected, screened and organised the information gathered in the area, which was then sent to the I.S.P.A. Headquarters; the latter forwarded it to the relevant superior bodies and planned any repressive action to be taken. At a later stage, the Turin and Milan Sectors were dissolved and their members, approximately fifty officers and agents, were transferred to a special Political Police Section specifically set up at the SS Polizeiführer Oberitalien West. The five Sectors made it possible to branch out the department's activities not only in Lombardy, but also in Piedmont, Liguria and Veneto.

For the delicate task to which they had been assigned, the two Mobile Units had been formed with elements of *'absolute faith and proven courage, with particular aptitude for repressive work'*, as they had to intervene in operations defined as 'emergency', following particular intelligence findings.

Commander of the I.S.P.A. was Questore Eugenio Pennacchio . As far as personnel administration was concerned, the Officers depended on the Public Security Officers' Personnel Division, while the Non-Commissioned Officers and Agents depended on the Autonomous Company of the General Directorate of Public Security; in addition to the remuneration proper to the Republican Police, the members of this Inspectorate were also entitled to the special allowance of the Political Police Division.

The planned staffing of the I.S.P.A. was 166 men:
- 15 Officials
- 12 Officers
- 66 NCOs
- 73 Graduates and Agents

In order to adequately equip the Inspectorate with weapons, on 24 September 1944 the Minister of the Interior Buffarini Guidi sent a request to the commander of the SS und Polizei in Italy, urging him to grant Questore Pennacchio the authorisation to purchase from the manufacturers:
"[...]
No. 80 Mitra-Moschetti 'Beretta';
No. 800 Loaders x 40 rounds per projectile;
No. 800 Hand Grenades;
No. 4 'Breda' heavy machine guns
Ammunition for Mitra-Moschetti, for 'Breda' machine guns, 'Beretta' pistols, in adequate quantities'.
A report by the commander of the Inspectorate, dated 12 October 1944, shows that at that date the actual number of men was 130:

- 20 Officials
- 66 NCOs
- 50 Graduates and Agents

to which were added about a hundred aspirants, who had applied to join the Ispettorato staff. At the same date, the network of informers numbered about 250 'trustees', who were present in all Italian regions under the control of the Social Republic.

The same report shows that the Brescia Mobile Nucleus, referred to in the document as the Mobile Nucleus of the I.S.P.A. Investigative Centre, had 35 men, coming from other investigative nuclei. The Turin Mobile Assault Nucleus, on the other hand, had 150 men and was to be quartered at the 'Cernaia' Barracks. The Nucleus was also being provided with armoured vehicles and civetta vehicles, i.e. civilian vehicles, equipped with camouflaged armour, to be used for patrols and political repression on the communication routes. Among the tasks of the Turin Assault Mobile Unit was also to be deployed during round-up operations conducted by other Republican Armed Forces units, with the specific task of political policing. On 3 October 1944, the Questore (Chief of Police) of Turin advocated the transfer of the I.S.P.A.'s Motorised Assault Nucleus to the High Commissioner for Piedmont, increasing its personnel and armament, to make it available as an emergency unit. From another document, it is noted that it was planned to reorganise the Assault Units according to this structure:

- Nucleus Command
- I Mobile Assault Unit
- II Mobile Assault Unit
- III Mobile Assault Unit

The following vehicles would be assigned to the Command Nucleus:
- 2 Torpedo cars
- 2 FIAT 1100 colonial, with armour, to be used as coquette vehicles
- 2 sidecars
- 4 motorbikes
- 1 bus
- 1 workshop truck
- 1 FIAT 626 truck with trailer
- 1 ambulance
- 1 motor vehicle armed with a heavy machine gun, to be used as an unmarked vehicle

Each of the 3 Assault Nuclei should have received:
- 1 Torpedo car
- 1 armoured SPA truck Dovunque, to be used as an unmarked vehicle
- 1 armoured car
- 1 motor vehicle armed with a heavy machine gun, to be used as an unmarked vehicle
- 2 shielded sidecars
- 6 motorbikes
- 2 armoured cars to be used as unmarked vehicles

It does not appear that these vehicles were actually assigned. Certainly at the beginning of 1945, at the I.S.P.A. Headquarters in Maderno (BS) there was a Motorised Nucleus, which had the following vehicles:

- 1 truck SPA Dovunque
- 1 armoured car of unidentified type
- 2 FIAT 1100 civil armoured cars

Towards the end of 1944, part of the personnel of the Piedmont and Liguria Sectors (5 officers, 21 non-commissioned officers and 23 agents) began to serve at Der SS Polizeifüehrer Obertialien-West, remaining under the command of Questore Pennacchio, probably following a request made on 16 October by General Tensfeld, who asked for the creation in Monza (or in its immediate vicinity) of an I.S.P.A. headquarters, which was to coordinate the activities of all the Sectors in direct contact with the German Command.

The Questura di Milano (Milan Police Headquarters) complained on numerous occasions about the actions of Questore Pennacchio, who used to suddenly arrive in the Lombard capital to carry out raids, detentions and arrests, without the local Questura being informed in advance and acting in a totally uncoordinated manner by the Milanese authorities.

From the testimony of members of the Inspectorate we learn that in November 1944, Questore Pennacchio set up an operational team, reporting directly to him, which operated in the rear of the southern front, especially in the Bologna area, and that, in the same period, the I.S.P.A. in Turin (in all probability, it was the Mobile Motorised Nucleus of the I.S.P.A.) was transformed into the Commissariat Information Service (S.I.C.), reporting directly to the High Commissioner for Piedmont, Zerbino.

Autonomous Mobile Legion "Ettore Muti"

The Autonomous Mobile Legion "Ettore Muti" in Milan, was a decidedly peculiar department, with an articulated structure and almost absolute autonomy, which was only formally included in the structure of the Republican Police.

After the Armistice, many Fascists from the dissolved Federations and Regional Groups got together and formed Action Squads; in Milan the phenomenon was particularly active and among the numerous Squads the "Ettore Muti" had a prodigious development, thanks to the zeal of its commander Franco Colombo. When the Republican Fascist Party decreed the dissolution of the Action Squads, the "Muti" had reached such a size and organization that it was decided to strengthen its police activity, placing it under the Ministry of the Interior. Thus, the Autonomous Mobile Legion "Ettore Muti" was created on March 18, 1944, engaged until the end of the war in political and military policing: anti-partisan, anti-guerrilla, anti-paratrooper, anti-reversal, but also in garrison duties, escorting vehicle and rail convoys, protection and defense.

The commander of the Legion was Franco Colombo, self-appointed Colonel, who assumed, for the Ministry of the Interior, the rank of Deputy Quartermaster.

The Legion carried out operational cycles with mobile units in Piedmont, Lombardy, Emilia and Liguria, as well as performing stationary garrison activities in and around Milan and on the Milan-Turin freeway, where it provided small garrisons to guard the freeway toll booths, with the task of making the transit of the important artery of communication safe. The Legion became infamous for the numerous roundups it carried out, for the torture and violence, perpetrated against suspects held at its Milan headquarters in Via Rovello, and for providing the firing squad, which slaughtered 15 partisans at Piazzale Loreto on August 10, 1944. After being taken from the San Vittore prison in Milan and being killed in retaliation for an attempt made on August 8, 1944, by unknown persons against a German truck on Viale Abruzzi in Milan, the bodies of the partisans were left exposed to the public and outraged for many, many hours, closely guarded by men of the "Muti" so that the bodies would not be moved by relatives[25]. According to the German authorities, the wretched action was supposed to have an intimidating character, and the fascist militiamen forced, guns in hand, the citizens in transit to witness the macabre "spectacle"[26].

It was the militiamen of the Autonomous Mobile Legion "Ettore Muti, in concert with agents of the Milan Republican Police Headquarters, who arrested the members of the Special Republican Police Department, the notorious "Koch Gang" on September 25, 1944, under the command of Questore Alberto Bettini.

The Legion's personnel ranged from 1,000 to 2,700 and had more than 260 fallen and more than 300 wounded. It ceased to exist between April 26 and 27, 1945.

Special Autonomous Departments

These were autonomous formations that were entrusted (or had autonomously entrusted themselves, as we shall see) with special investigative, informational and repressive tasks toward any activity deemed politically subversive. Some of these units, such as the Special Republican Police Department (also known as the "Koch Gang," after the name of its commander, Lieutenant Pietro Koch) or the Special Services Department (known as the "Carità Gang," headed by Major Mario Carità) operated in close relationship with the Germanic Armed Forces and were only nominally framed within the Republican Police Corps, enjoying wide operational independence. For this reason, these gangs constituted de facto irregular formations, which operated in an extremely violent manner, without any duty to the official chain of command of the Republican Police, so much so that Benito Mussolini himself, after being repeatedly informed of the heinous acts committed, ordered the disbandment of some of these units, as was the case, for example, with the Koch Gang. As proof of this hostility of Mussolini toward these formations, on September 25, 1944, Secondo Larice, formerly the auxiliary Questore of Venice, arrived in Milan as Inspector of Public Security for the entirety of the assignment given him directly by the Duce to "dismantle" all the special police operating in the city, such as, for example, the "Koch" Band. The Republican Police proved quite intolerant of these units that acted on the fringes of legality, so much so that Pietro Koch had to complain several times about the behavior shown by the Police officers commanded to lend aid to his unit during raids or other operations, calling them "indolent," a behavior voluntarily held, because the Police did not want to have anything to do with the atrocities carried out by these elements. The Germans also showed signs of impatience with these units, despite the fact that they were more or less directly dependent precisely on the Germanic authorities (especially the SD), which, at times, provided them with concrete support in terms of arms and means. Indeed, harassing attitudes such as trafficking in seized property, conducted by members of these "auxiliary" police, were judged reprehensible by the Germans themselves. Instances were not uncommon in which informers from these "special" departments played double or triple game, offering their "services" to several departments at once, departments which in turn found themselves really operating in a state of competition with each other, so much so that they often made arrests of informers from other units, in order to have a free field.

Special Autonomous Company of the Auxiliary Police (CAS)

Commanded by Captain Renato Tartarotti, it was organized in Bologna in June 1944, following the dissolution of the local Auxiliary Police Battalion. The Company was stationed at the residence

---

25 Among the victims was a member of the Republican Police, guard Emidio Mastrodomenico, serving at the Lambiate Police Station, who had been linked to the Resistance.
26 Just in response to this terrible "macabre dance," the following year the corpses of Benito Mussolini, Claretta Petacci and 18 Fascist hierarchs were exposed to public ridicule at the same place.

of the Questore of Bologna himself, Villa Campanati on Via Siepelunga 67[27], and became a sort of "second police headquarters," dealing with political facts, administratively autonomous but functionally dependent on Questore Giovanni Tebaldi.

The C.A.S. carried out not only the service of the Quaestor's Bodyguard, but also engaged extensively in operations aimed at weakening and damaging the partisan movement, even using unorthodox methods and inflicting terrible torture during the extremely harsh interrogations to which those suspected of colluding with the resistance movement were subjected, enjoying immunity and "right to loot," that is, the freedom to loot homes and stores that smelled of rebellion. The C.A.S. also had a Flying Squad known as "the red truck," which specialized in street executions.

The Special Autonomous Company was moved to Trieste, in September 1944, following the transfer of Questore Tebaldi to the Julian city and the bad relations between Captain Tartarotti and the new Questore of Bologna Fabiani. With the transfer, the C.A.S. lost its operational autonomy and, in a short time, was also deprived of its commander, who was arrested following a complaint concerning the financial management of the corps and imprisoned in Brescia prison, from which he managed to escape, however.

When the war ended, on May 16, some fifteen Bolognese fascists who were attempting to escape were tracked down and captured in Val Trompia, including Captain Renato Tartarotti himself and other men of the Special Autonomous Company. Tried for violence, murder and theft, Tartarotti was sentenced to death by firing squad in the back by the Extraordinary Court of Assizes in Bologna on July 4, 1945, the only death sentence carried out in the Emilian city. In the course of Tartarotti's trial, it emerged how the unit not only engaged in violent repression of partisans, but was also guilty of "common" crimes such as aggravated robberies, requisitions and extortion against ordinary citizens, taking advantage of the breakdown of the city's sociopolitical fabric.

Special Services Department - "Charity Band"

Officially known as the Special Services Department, the "Banda Carità" took its name from its commander Mario Carità, an M.V.S.N. Centurion, originally from Milan but transplanted to Florence in 1936, who after the Armistice organized this unit within the reconstituted XCII Militia Legion, with the task of annihilating the enemies of Republican Fascism, both external such as partisans and internal such as traitors.

In Florence, the Band depended on the Command Company of the Legion and, after several moves, took its headquarters at 67 Via Bolognese, in what would become known as "Villa Triste," for the ill-treatment to which prisoners were subjected. The "Charity" achieved relevant results against the Florentine Resistance, following, unfortunately, vicious methods of repression.

In July 1944 the Band was transferred to Bergantino (RO) and then to Padua, where it acquired a marked operational autonomy, seizing important successes, especially the dismantling of the G.A.P. network in the city and province, cooperating closely with the SS Command in the square.

At the Liberation, many elements of the Band attempted to escape to safety by joining the retreating German troops to the north, but many were captured, tried in two separate proceedings (the first in Padua in October 1945 and the second in Lucca, in 1951) and sentenced to prison terms. Mario Carità, on the other hand, was killed in Siusi on May 19, 1945 in a firefight with Allied soldiers.

---

[27] Villa Campanati thus became infamous with the nickname "Villa Triste" because of the vicious tortures and executions that were the order of the day there. Captain Tartarotti also used to inflict harsh punishments on his officers if they refused to obey his violent orders.

Special Republican Police Department - "Koch Gang"

The Koch gang was a Special Squad, whose official name was Reparto Speciale di Polizia Repubblicana, active between December 1943 and June 1944 in Rome, when it moved to Milan following the arrival of the Allies, where it operated until the end of the war. The Department, which was infamous for the violence and cruelty used during interrogations, was named after its commander Pietro Koch . The latter, who had been recalled to the Grenadiers in the spring of 1943, was caught in the Armistice in Livorno and from there moved to Florence, where he joined the newly formed Republican Fascist Party, enlisting in Mario Carità's "Special Security Department." Koch immediately proved unscrupulous and arrested Colonel Marino, aide to Army General Mario Caracciolo di Feroleto, former commander of the 5th Army who had attempted to defend Florence from the Germans during the tragic days of the Armistice. Koch thus learned that the General had taken refuge in Rome at the Vatican convent of San Sebastiano, in the guise of a Franciscan friar, under the tutelage of Giuseppe Cordero Lanza di Montezemolo.

In December 1943 Koch took himself to Rome, to present himself to Republican Police Chief Tamburini, reporting that he was aware of General Caracciolo's hiding place and was instructed to arrest him. Koch carried out the operation without delay, violating Vatican extraterritoriality, and the arrest of Army General Mario Caracciolo di Feroleto also made it possible to find a memorial signed by the General, a most interesting document that contained unequivocal information regarding the events that led to the fall of Fascism and accusations against Mussolini.

As a result of the results obtained, in January 1944 the Chief of Police authorized the formation of what was to be the staff of the department under Koch's orders, which was to be oriented toward the repression of any activity contrary to the policies of the Social Republic and Germany. the "Band" thus assumed this organization in January 1944:

- Command Office
- Office of Investigation and Information;
- Office of Operations;
- Secretarial Office, liaison, accounting;
- Legal Department;
- Operations department.

This Police Department, which took the official name of Special Republican Police Department, immediately began its activities in the purely political field; it was also joined by several elements of the Band Carità, reaching the size of about seventy men, including some priests. The Department's first headquarters was at the Open City SS Headquarters at 115 Via Tasso, but shortly afterwards the Band moved to 2 Via Principe Amedeo, at the Oltremare boarding house, where it occupied three united apartments, one of which served as an interrogation room, conducted with brutal methods. In short order, the Koch Gang once again came to prominence for the capture of Giovanni Roveda, Chairman of the Central Committee of the Italian Communist Party: it was the first operation carried out in the Capital in which specialized Italian-German police forces participated.

Toward the end of January 1944, a large raid was carried out against the Action Party in Rome, with the aim of crushing it just as it was strengthening its organization, an operation that led to numerous arrests and the seizure of a printing press that was clandestinely printing the party's newspaper. The Koch Band was subsequently engaged in fighting two armed nuclei of partisans, operating around Rome, in the Tor Sapienza area, arresting almost all of the elements and seizing a large loot of weapons and ammunition; 21 of those arrested were later shot at the Fosse Ardeatine.

On the night of Feb. 3-4, the unit stormed the convent attached to St. Paul's Basilica, where numerous Jews, draft dodgers, former police officers and high-ranking soldiers of the Royal Army, including Generals Monti and Fortunato, had taken refuge, arresting a total of 67 people.

After winning through stratagems the trust of some Patriotic Action Groups of the Communist Party, the Koch Gang carried out numerous raids that led to the arrest of more than 200 members of the Roman Resistance and made it possible to foil some important attacks planned by the partisans themselves against electrical installations and against the Germanic Commands in the Capital. Following the Via Rasella bombing, the command headquarters was no longer deemed adequate, and the unit occupied the Jaccarino boarding house at 38 Via Romagna on April 21. Koch, through numerous arrests and violent interrogations, managed to reconstruct the dynamics of the bombing and the names of the perpetrators, informing General Kurt Mälzer, commander of the Wehrmacht. Koch's methods were advocated by Kappler's SS, and the gang collaborated with the SS Command at Via Tasso, even going so far as to procure for Kappler some names to be placed on the list of those sentenced to death in retaliation for the Via Rasella bombing. For these violent and hasty methods, Koch was first warned not to remain in Rome, was then "strongly advised" not to return to the capital from Florence, and finally was even threatened with arrest by Fascist elements and even by the SS, who opposed his conduct that was absolutely outside all rules. A number of common thugs, such as Guglielmo Blasi, a notorious thief in the capital, were also enlisted among the ranks of the Unit. Arrested in flagrante delicto, he saved himself from a possible death sentence (original SS documents, including an identification card, were found on him) by revealing to Questore Caruso that he was aware of the plan the G.A.P. had devised to kill him. Entrusted to Koch, Blasi became part of the Koch Department and, thanks to his delusions, led to the total annihilation of central G.A.P. led by Franco Calamandrei and Carlo Salinari and to having Carlo Salinari, Franco Calamandrei, Raul Falcioni, Duilio Grigioni, Luigi Pintor and Silvio Serra arrested. He eventually became Koch's own bodyguard.

After the Allies entered Rome in June 1944, the Koch Gang moved to Milan, where they took up residence at Villa Fossati, between Via Paolo Uccello and Via Masaccio, which would later be referred to in the city as "Villa Triste." Equipped with barbed-wire fencing, searchlights and sirens, the villa was turned into a place of detention and pain, and some rooms were turned into torture chambers. Also joining the Ward in Milan were actor Osvaldo Valenti, who soon became a liaison man between Koch and Prince Borghese of the 10th MAS, count-industrialist Guido Stampa and a number of women. The gang's torture methods and interrogation techniques became infamous and almost codified, as violence was perpetrated in a systematic manner.

According to a report pertaining to the "Police Organs Functioning in Milan"[28] Koch's department in Milan had "[...] *a very large, luxuriously furnished premises with attached prisons that can house up to 70 inmates. Dr. Koch*[29] *is assisted by about ten officials and an unspecified number of permanent officers (about fifty). Around the organization also gravitates a complex of confidants, informants, etc. chosen from the various walks of life.*" The report goes on to lament the difficulty of being able to carry out a control action on Koch's work: "*Given the system of operation of the Department (absolute impenetrability even toward the Police Headquarters in the preparation and execution of*

---

[28] Photostatic copy in possession of the author.
[29] Koch was not actually a graduate; he had attended law school, without reaching the conclusion. However, it was taken to be the custom to call him Doctor, as is commonly done for all Public Security Officers (who are in fact really graduates).

operations as well as in the subsequent investigative period) any control action is very problematic." Soon the Department was assigned other tasks, such as carrying out internal investigations into the governing and political bodies of the R.S.I., which were aimed at identifying bangs out of control or even hostile to the regime. These investigations decreed the beginning of the decline of the Koch Band: in fact, when the Department's operations began to affect the "Muti" Legion, the leadership group of Colombo's unit felt threatened and succeeded in obtaining the Duce's consent to dismantle the Koch Department. Thus, on September 25, 1944, a forceful action was carried out by the Autonomous Mobile Legion Ettore Muti, under the command of Questore Alberto Bettini and elements of the Milan Republican Police Headquarters: Villa Fossati was surrounded, about fifty members of the Band were arrested, all the accumulated loot was seized and the command was temporarily taken over by Major Folli of the "Muti" Legion. Koch was arrested on December 17 and locked up in San Vittore prison in Milan. Later, despite Kappler's protests, the Unit was dismantled. Some members of the gang were executed in the days following the April 25 uprising, others were sentenced to prison terms and returned to freedom in the early 1950s. Koch, on the other hand, had managed to escape on April 25, 1945, from San Vittore and took refuge in Florence, but on June 1 he spontaneously presented himself at the Questura in the Tuscan capital. Tried in Rome, he was sentenced to death and the sentence was carried out on June 5, 1945 in Fort Bravetta[30].

Special Auxiliary Police Department "Tupin"
In the summer of 1944, Enrico Vezzalini was appointed as the new Chief of the Province of Novara, replacing Gaspero Barbero. From Ferrara, Vezzalini reached the Piedmontese city on July 22, together with the "Giorgi" Auxiliary Company, formally dependent on the G.N.R., but better known as the "Tupin" (an acronym for "Tutti Uniti Per l'Italia Nostra"), a veritable personal Guard of the Prefect. Commanded by Captain Tortonesi, the "Tupins" took up residence at 15 Monte San Gabriele Street, received orders only and directly from Vezzalini, were reinforced with a score of young men enlisted in the city called "Tupicin"[31], and soon became infamous in the Novara area for the ferocity they used in repressing partisans and suspects. The "Tupin" also participated in the round of operations that led to the recapture, by R.S.I. units, of Valdossola. The unit formally came under the Ministry of the Interior, taking the name Special Department of Auxiliary Police "Tupin" and, later, 1st Department of Arditi Auxiliary Police, but without losing ferocity. In fact, in August the Provincial Command of the G.N.R. of Ferrara had requested the return of the Tortonesi Company to the city, but, through Vezzalini's intervention, the department was transferred to the formal dependence of the Ministry of the Interior, assuming the new name of Special Department of Auxiliary Police "Tupin," while continuing to be subject exclusively to the direction of the Prefect of Novara.

In Novara the "Tupins" sadly distinguished themselves by their ferocity, also conducting anti-partisan actions in the province, and while in the city the unit had 3 casualties. On August 29, 1944, the "Tupins" conducted a roundup in the area of Arizzano (VB) in collaboration with a unit of the 6th Verbania Company of the Novara Black Brigade, under the orders of Marshal Vittorio Scavini. On

---
30 Given the character's fame, the authorities saw fit to document the execution with a filmed shot. Exceptional director wanted to be Luchino Visconti, who in turn had been arrested and tortured by Koch.
31 These were young people from the "Goffredo Mameli" Youth Action Group.

Sept. 12, however, together with officers of the so-called "Squadraccia" (another para-police unit of the Novara Police Headquarters), about 40 squad members of the Novara Black Brigade de about 20 German soldiers from the Gendarmerie Zug in Novara, the "Tupins" led an attack along the Arona - Invorio -Gozzano road, aimed at ridding the village of Gozzano of the partisan presence. The action then ended with a roundup towards Omegna (VB) and Gravellona Toce (VB). A few days later, on Sept. 20, a training unit consisting of squads from the 1st Battalion of the Black Brigade "Cristina" of Novara and the Special Police Unit "Tupin," carried out a roundup in the Strona Valley, in the course of which militiamen Boari Alfredo, Chiacchio Giuseppe and Fabbri Giuseppe of the "Tupin" were killed in a firefight near Crusinallo. The two units were later joined by a column made up of Black Brigade squads and officers of the Novara Republican Police, commanded by Questore Pasqualy. Over the course of the autumn a sharp disagreement between Prefect Vezzalini and Questore Pasqualy deepened, often resulting in acts of open hostility.

The "Tupins" also participated in the operations to recapture Valdossola (Operation Avanti), between October 9 and November 4, 1944. On October 29, some 30 officers and soldiers, who had distinguished themselves during Operation "Avanti," were received in Gargnano by Mussolini, including Captain Tortonesi, Sergeant Nardi, Marshal Chierici, Corporal Camattari, and soldiers Pennoncini and Poggi of the Police Arditi "Tupin" Unit. At the end of operations in Domodossola, a detachment of the "Tupin" unit under the orders of Lieutenant Duner was deployed and remained garrisoned until the end of December.

As an illustration of the bad reputation the unit had created for us, on Oct. 23 militiaman Sturaro Emilio was picked up by partisans near Bellinzago (NO), who disappeared into thin air and has since been listed as missing; the same end was met by militiaman Penoncini Giovanni, picked up in Vogogna (VB) on Nov. 4.

Beginning on December 14, 1944, the "Tupins" participated in a new major roundup in the area between the towns of Borgomanero, Borgoticino, Oleggio, and Fara, where groups of partisans from the "Osella" and "Nello" Brigades were located.

Following the removal of Vezzalini as head of the Province, the Tupins" were" removed from Novara in early January 1945, moving initially to Milan and later to Emilia-Romagna, moved to the dependencies of the Mobile Black Brigade "Attilio Pappalardo," born in Bologna on September 1, 1944, forming the Armored Company "Tupin," equipped with at least 2 armored cars.

Police Assault Department (R.A.P.)

It depended on the Bologna Police Headquarters and was commanded by Captain Alberto Noli. It had not only public security duties, but also polite (and therefore anti-partisan) police duties; it was based in Piazza Galileo, where cells were equipped for harsh detention. Some of the unit's members came from the local Compagnia della Morte, formed in the capital of Emilia by the Republican Fascist Party, under the command of Captain Alceste Porcelli The Unit took part in numerous anti-partisan operations in the city, eliminating many components of the Bolognese Resistance.

A nucleus of two hundred men, including R.A.P. agents and Black Brigades militiamen, surrounded the university, where a cell of the Action Party had been formed, on the morning of October 20, 1944. When machine gun fire was opened against the Athenaeum, some partisans managed to escape, but, after a couple of hours of battle, the resistance fighters still barricaded in the institution were snatched away and captured one by one. Five of the captured partisans were shot immediately in the courtyard of the Rector's Office.

On Nov. 7, 1944, 50 officers of the Police Assault Unit took part in a roundup operation, together with 150 men of the Black Brigades and 50 of the Feldgendarmerie, an activity that led to the identification of an important partisan base at the Municipal Slaughterhouse. A violent battle, known as the "Battle of Porta Lame," was unleashed, considered the most important among those conducted in an urban center between partisans and Nazi-fascists. In the course of the clashes Police Assault Unit officer Eliseo Zanosi died.

At the end of the war many officers of the Police Assault Unit tried to get to safety by leaving Bologna. On June 4, 1945 some officers were captured along with former Prefect Dino Fantozzi.

Political Information Center (C.I.P.)

It was established in Milan on Sept. 23, 1944, with headquarters at 14 Fatebenefratelli Street; manager of the Center was Dr. Mario Finizio, self-appointed Questore, to whom some 40 men answered. The Political Information Center essentially carried out financial control operations, reporting to the SS and was divided into a Male Section, headed by Finizio himself, and a Female Section, headed by his wife. Finizio had presented himself in Milan with credentials provided by the Chief of Police himself, calling himself Quaestor, appointments that in reality never seem to have officially occurred.

The C.I.P. forged very close relations with the Germanic Police, almost of direct dependence on it; Finizio, moreover, very often went to talk to the Chief of Police in Vobarno, to communicate to him all the information gathered by his men, information that was not shared with any other organ of the Republican Police. The C.I.P. executive, moreover, managed to create for himself a dense network of informers, who were paid handsomely, directly by Finizio himself, who drew on his vast economic resources. The Center was subsequently disbanded on authority and Finizio placed in detention, as he often operated unjustified seizures of goods and valuables, which were then reused for exclusively personal use by the unit's members, and it turns out that five of its members[32] asked to be allowed to transfer to the Republican Police force[33]. The Questura Mobile Squad, which was in charge of disbanding the unit and investigating its work, recovered large quantities of seized goods stored at various warehouses, scattered throughout the city[34].

Special Police Services

The Ministry of the Interior organized two Special Police Service Groups, intended for sensitive tasks, such as sabotage operations in territory already occupied by the Anglo-Americans. A first Group was deployed in the Milan area, under the cover name of a perfume company, and consisted of military personnel from the Air Force and the Militia, The second Group, on the other hand, was

---

32 The department's staff had been reduced to 22 personnel.

33 It is documented that these elements made requests to Questore Mario Bassi for exorbitant monthly pay (10,000 liras at the time) and cash rewards for any recoveries and seizures made.

34 From a report, undated but probably written by the Milan Police Headquarters at the end of 1944, it appears that other characters and groups were operating in the Lombard capital, officially linked to the Republican Police, but in fact carrying out activities that were not very lawful. Among them was one such Questore Gastone De Larderel, who presented himself in July 1944 to the Questore of Milan, with credentials provided by the Deputy Chief of Police, which attributed to him unspecified "special assignments," which in fact resulted in a dissolute and wasteful life; against this self-styled Police official, the Venice Police Headquarters possessed serious elements (De Larderel later went over to the Resistance). There was also such a Miranda Serra, a madam who provided information service, through 5 prostitutes placed in her employ, on behalf of the High Commissioner for the Veneto Giuseppe Pizzirani, who was dealing, among other things, with the reorganization of the Special Police Departments.

formed exclusively by Republican Police personnel under the command of Questore Del Zoppo; this group was given special security assignments under the direct reports of the Prime Minister's Office. The activity of this second Group continued, obviously under the strictest cover, until June 1945, succeeding in rescuing members of the first Group captured by partisans.

Special Inspectorate

This was none other than the department known, prior to the Armistice, by the name of Ispettorato Speciale di Pubblica Sicurezza per la Venezia Giulia (I.S.P.G./V.G.), which had been organized in 1942 in Trieste, intended for the fight against the repression of anti-fascist movements and the search for foreign partisans in the vast area from Gorizia to Fiume, when the activity of the Slovenian partisan bands was beginning to become more intense. It was the only structure exclusively dedicated to this purpose in the Kingdom of Italy and was composed not only of men from the Royal Corps of Public Security Agents, but also of elements of the Royal Carabinieri, the Royal Guardia di Finanza and the M.V.S.N. Confinaria, specifically trained in innovative tactics, with modern armament and organized into motorized nuclei. The inspectorate was under the orders of Inspector General Giuseppe Gueli, who made nonchalant use of unorthodox methods and torture against arrested anti-fascists. Among his employees became infamous for ferocity Deputy Commissioner Gaetano Collotti . After July 25, 1943, Prime Minister Pietro Badoglio disbanded the Inspectorate, but assigned Gueli the delicate task of guarding Mussolini after his arrest.

After the Armistice, the unit resumed its activities against anti-fascists in the Trieste area, but, being placed in practice under the control of the SS Trieste command, it was also overbearingly concerned with the persecution of Jews. Two elements of the Inspectorate, the aforementioned Gaetano Collotti and Marshal Sigfrido Mazzuccato, stood out overbearingly in this phase.

Collotti created the eponymous "Banda Collotti," which in the summer of 1944 was guilty of repeated executions of civilians, who were thrown into a mine shaft in Basovizza; Collotti himself personally tortured anti-fascist prisoners. At the end of the war Collotti was captured by members of the Resistance at Olmi di San Biagio di Callalta (TV), while together with some of his agents, his pregnant fiancée and a substantial cargo of gold, he attempted to escape. Transferred to the Cartiera di Mignagola paper mill, Collotti, his fiancée and his agents were executed by partisans commanded by Gino Simionato, known as "Falco," during a mass shooting of R.S.I. soldiers and civilians who were openly fascist.

Mazzuccato, at the behest of Rijeka Prefect Tamburini, formed an auxiliary police unit dedicated to anti-fascist repression, whose headquarters were located on San Michele Street, known at the time as the "Olivares squad"; most of the gang's 200 or so members had been co-opted from among local convicts. The unit was disbanded in September 1944 by German authorities, and Mazzucato was sent to Germany to Buchenwald.

Instead, Giuseppe Gueli was sentenced, for the crime of collaborationism alone, to eight years in prison, a sentence suspended under the "Togliatti" amnesty.

▲ Elements of Rome's Mobile Public Security Battalion in front of Rome's Regina Coeli prison during a prisoner uprising. The policemen are supported by some L3 tanks and an AS42 truck; however, the image probably dates back to July 1944, after the Allied occupation of the capital, when the dissolved Italian Africa Police ceded its armoured vehicles, L6/40 tanks and AS42 trucks of the Metropolitano type, to the Police (Crippa).

▼ Republican Police armoured truck, used by partisans after the liberation. It was probably used by a department of the Armed Police Forces, such as the I.S.P.A., which had its own Motorised Nucleus, or by another unit, such as the Turin Instruction Battalion, which had an armoured truck on an SPA chassis.

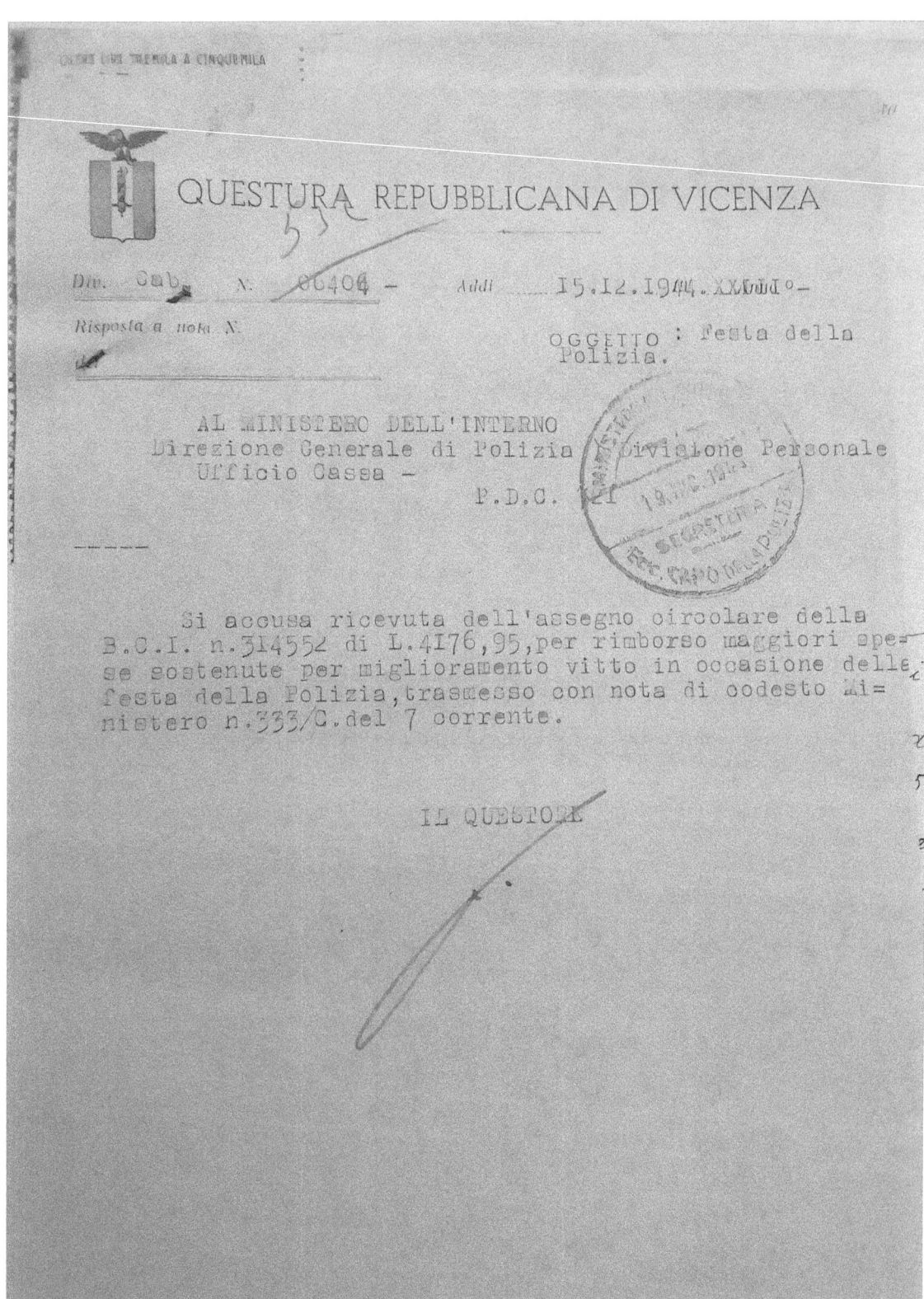

▲ Receipt for the cashing of a cheque from the Questura Repubblicana di Vicenza (WEB source).

QUESTURA REPUBBLICANA DI VICENZA

Comando Reparto Agenti Polizia Ausiliaria

Prot. N. .... Vicenza, li 9/4/1945/XXIII°

Risposta al foglio N. .... del ....

OGGETTO: D I C H I A R A Z I O N E

    Si dichiara che l'Agente FAGGIONATO Bruno fu Agostino dal giorno 5/I/1945 al giorno 7/4/45 ha prestato regolare servizio presso questo Reparto.
    Si rilascia la presente a richiesta dell'interessato ad uso amministrativo.

IL COMANDANTE DEL BATTAGLIONE
(Magg. Arturo Pertegato)

▲ The header of this document from the last days of the war is interesting: Comando Reparto Agenti Polizia Ausiliaria della Questura di Vicenza (WEB source).

▲ Benito Mussolini visiting the headquarters of the Autonomous Mobile Legion 'Ettore Muti' in Via Rovello in Milan in December 1944, during what became known as the 'Milanese days of the Duce'. On his left is his chief escort, Republican Police Captain Mario Nudi, wearing the typical uniform of the Corps, used by officers during the Social Republic (he appears to wear the two-coloured flames used by the Arditi of the 'Caruso' Legion on his jacket).

▲ The building that housed the Turin Police Headquarters was attacked and then looted during the uprising of 25 April 1945.

▼ The plaque commemorating the slaughter of 665 Gorizians in Gorizia, who were deported, infoibrated or drowned at the end of the war. The city was strenuously defended by the officers of the Republican Police, who paid a very high tribute of blood for their resistance to the Tito partisans.

▲ Vice Brigadier Felice Sena, in force at the Political Squad of the Verona Police Headquarters, in a post-war photograph, when he served in the re-established Police of the Italian Republic. Vice-brigadier Sena was the protagonist in the rescue of around 300 Jews from Verona, whose unorthodox interventions managed to save them from Nazi persecution.

26 Feb 45

MINISTERO DELL'INTERNO
Polizia Repubblicana
Comando Forze Armate

Vobarno 20 Marzo 1945 XXIII

Per l'inserzione nel Quaderno di Ordini =

Alla Segreteria Particolare
dell'Ecc.il Capo della Polizia
<u>Milano</u>

VITTIME DEL DOVERE
―――――――――――――

Guardia Polizia BALDUCCI CATALDO, effettivo alla Questura di Torino, ucciso il 26 Febbraio u.s. da un fuori legge.

(Pier Luigi Pansera)

▲ Communication issued by the Armed Police Forces Command, signed by Regent Prefect Pier Luigi Pansera (WEB source).

▲ Group of NCOs of the Republican Police: one can see all the features of the typical uniforms of the R.S.I. period, such as the beret frieze, the chest badge, the amaranth square insignia with gladius.

▼ Quaestor of Rome Pietro Caruso, after whom the Police Arditi Legion was named.

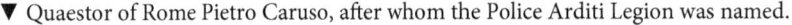

Il generale Montagna costituisce la Legione Arditi della Polizia "P. Caruso"

MILANO, 27 novembre.

In un cortile della Questura il Capo della Polizia generale Montagna ha tenuto rapporto ai funzionari ed agli agenti.

Dopo aver passato in rassegna i vari reparti, il generale Montagna ha dettato le direttive da seguire nel delicato compito affidato alla Polizia.

Al rapporto presenziava un reparto con musica della Legione Autonoma « Ettore Muti ».

Successivamente il generale Montagna ha dichiarato costituita la Legione Arditi della Polizia «Pietro Caruso» il cui primo reparto ha poi sfilato per le vie della città destando viva ammirazione per il marziale impeccabile comportamento.

▲ An article appeared in the newspaper 'Il Popolo del Friuli' of Monday 27 November 1944, announcing the establishment of the 'Caruso' (Maressi) Police Arditi Legion in Milan.

▲ Postcard published for the 'Pietro Caruso' Legion: in the iconic depiction of the Ardito, one can see some details of the uniform, typical of this unit, such as the two-coloured two-pointed flames and the Ardito badge, worn on the left arm, made, however, on crimson cloth (and not green, as for the Army). Behind it is the profile of Milan Cathedral, the city where the unit was born and operated.

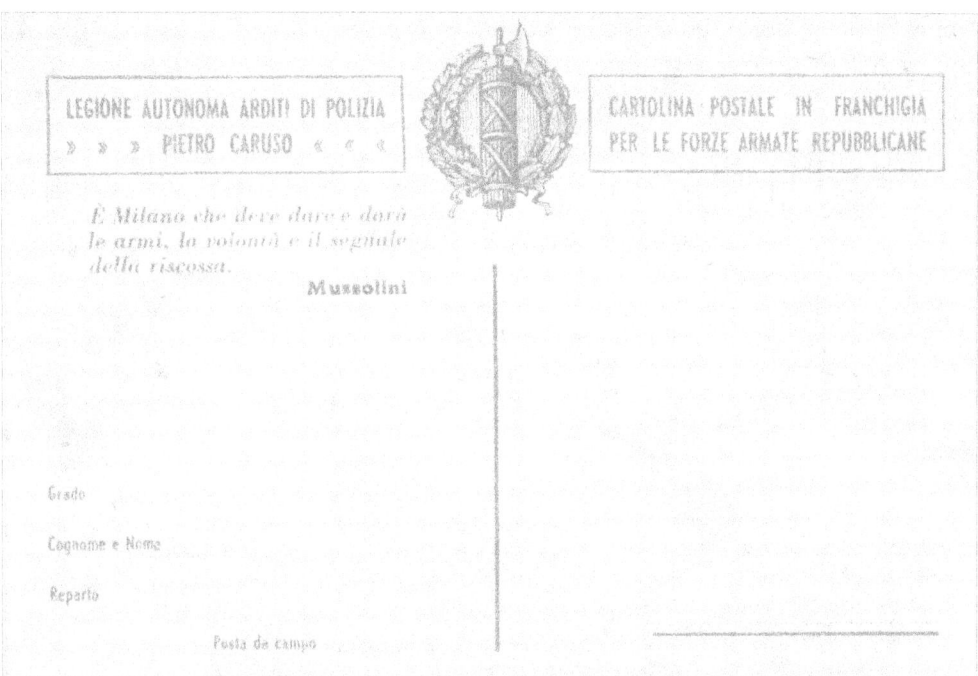

▲ Back of the postcard issued for the Legione Arditi di Polizia 'Pietro Caruso' (Police Armed Forces Legion 'Pietro Caruso'); there is a sentence by Mussolini, who, in the last periods of the Social Republic, insistently emphasised the primary role that would fall to the Lombard capital for the rebirth of Fascism.

▼ Group of soldiers of the Republican Police: these are most probably Arditi of the 'Caruso' Legion. Interesting is the frieze painted on the left side of the helmet, which recalls the breast badge of the Republican Police; this detail has been misinterpreted by some scholars as the frieze of the Italian SS Legion, but the handwriting is evidently different.

PREFETTURA REPUBBLICANA DI MILANO

Divisione Polizia

N. 02094
Risp. Nota N.

Milano, 1° Febbraio 1945
XXIII

OGGETTO

AL COMANDANTE REGIONALE MILITARE DI

MILANO.

Il Duce con provvedimento in data 31 Gennaio c.a. ha accolto l'istanza di grazia nei confronti di :

1°) BESCAPE' CESARE di Giuseppe
2°) DORIGO CARLA fu Alessandro
3°) DOLCI CARLO di Giacomo

commutando la pena di morte in 20 anni di reclusione.

Di conseguenza la sentenza di morte è eseguibile nei confronti di :

1°) MANTOVANI VENERINO fu Antonio
2°) RESTI VITTORIO fu Angelo
3°) CAMPEGGI LUIGI di Giuseppe
4°) MANDELLI FRANCO di Giovanni
5°) VOLPONES OLIVIERO fu Guglielmo
6°) COLOMBO PIETRO fu Guglielmo
7°) RONCHI LUIGI di Matteo
8°) PELLEGATTA RENATO di Luigi
9°) MOTTA ALDO di Vincenzo
10°) CEREDA EMILIO di Danilo.

IL CAPO DELLA PROVINCIA

▲ Document from the Republican Prefecture of Milan, sanctioning the execution of capital punishment for 10 partisans; 3 others had managed to obtain a pardon from Mussolini (WEB source).

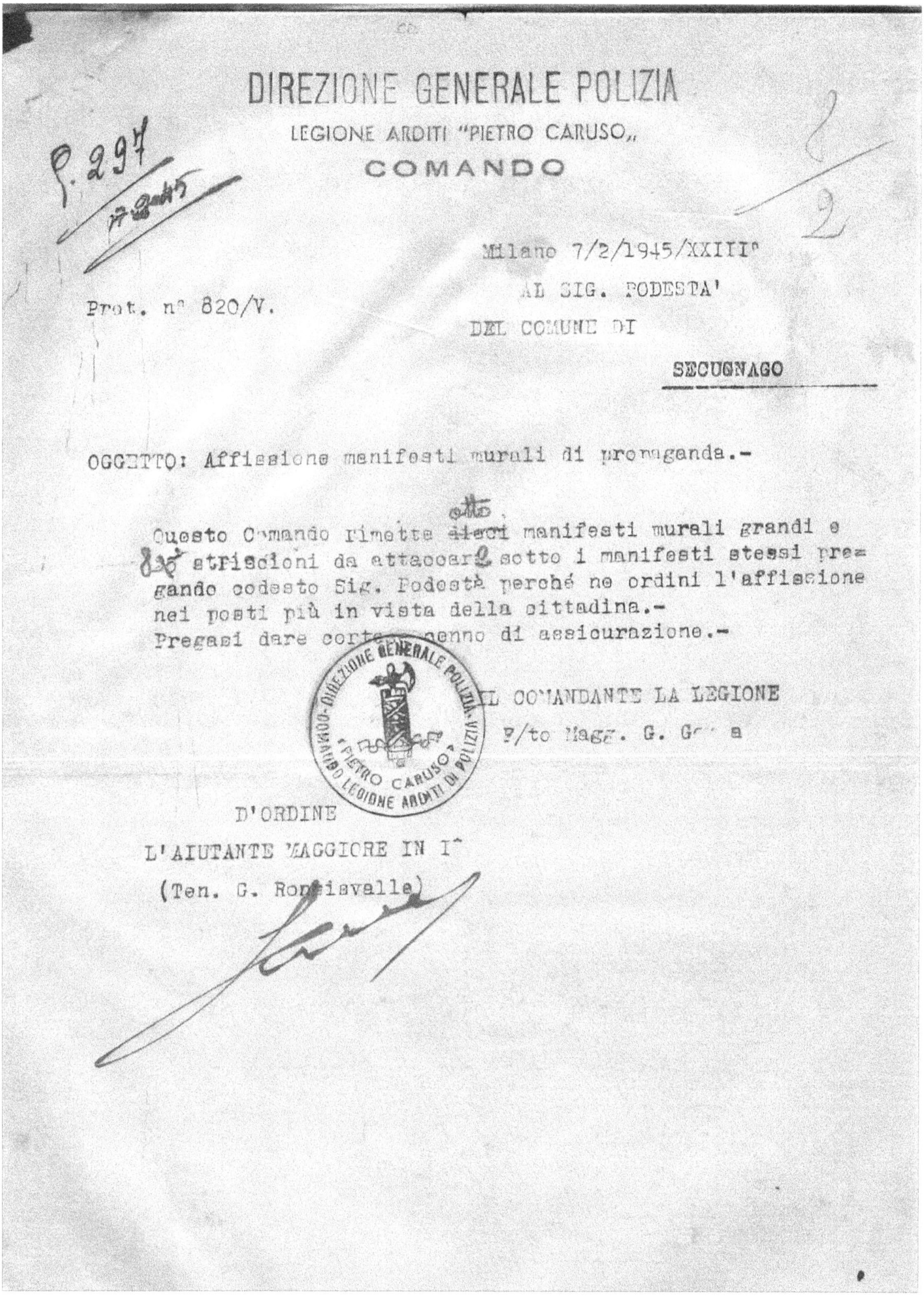

DIREZIONE GENERALE POLIZIA
LEGIONE ARDITI "PIETRO CARUSO"
COMANDO

P. 297

Prot. n° 820/V.

Milano 7/2/1945/XXIII°

AL SIG. PODESTA'
DEL COMUNE DI

SECUGNAGO

OGGETTO: Affissione manifesti murali di propaganda.-

Questo Comando rimette otto manifesti murali grandi e striscioni da attaccare sotto i manifesti stessi pregando codesto Sig. Podestà perché ne ordini l'affissione nei posti più in vista della cittadina.-
Pregasi dare cortese cenno di assicurazione.-

IL COMANDANTE LA LEGIONE
F/to Magg. G. G...a

D'ORDINE
L'AIUTANTE MAGGIORE IN 1°
(Ten. G. Roncisvalle)

▲ Rare document of the Police Armed Forces Legion 'Pietro Caruso', interesting because it bears the header stamp of the Command and the round stamp of the Legion and the signature of the Adjutant First Lieutenant, Lieutenant Roncisvalle (WEB source).

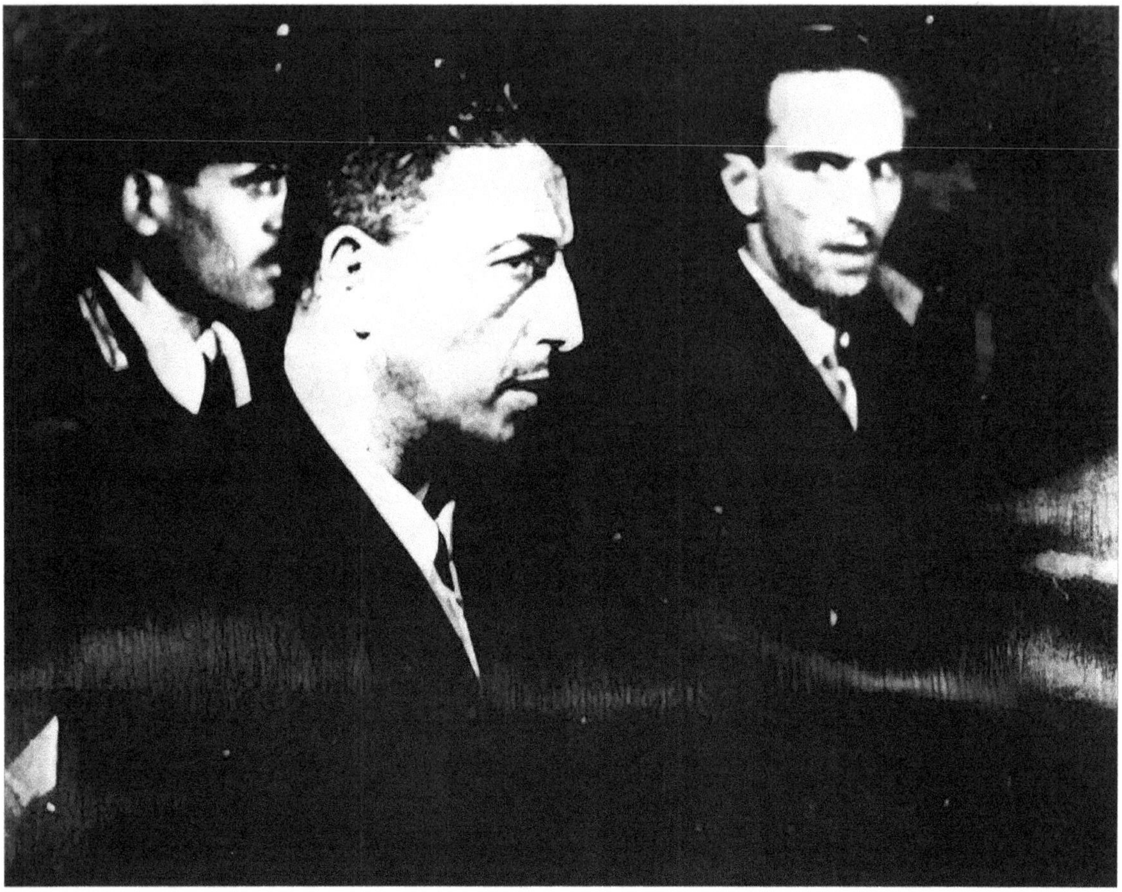

▲ Pietro Caruso during his trial in September 1944, which earned him the death sentence.

▼ Round stamp of the Ispettorato Speciale Polizia Anti Partigiani (I.S.P.A.), affixed on a document, next to the signature of the unit commander, Questore Eugenio Pennacchio (WEB source).

F.to (Que

p. c. c.
IL DIRIGENTE L'ISPETTORATO
(Questore E. Pennacchio)

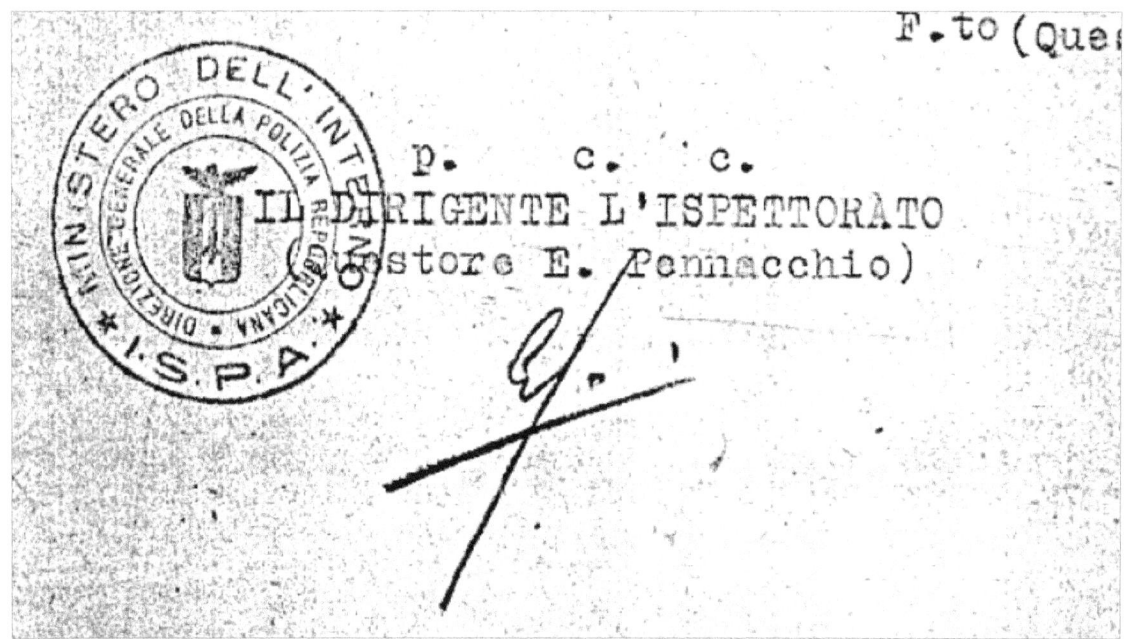

ACTIVITIES ON BEHALF OF JEWS AND POLITICAL PERSECUTED PEOPLE

The two-year period of the Civil War in Italy was an extremely difficult and troubled time. The Republican Police was an organism that did not go immune to the tsunami that invested not only all strata of the population, but also all civil and military apparatuses. If on the one hand, in fact, within the Republican Police were organized, as seen in the previous chapters, armed departments trained and destined specifically for the fight against the opponents of the regime, whether they were political opponents, Jews or ordinary citizens, on the other hand, it cannot be forgotten how numerous members of the Police did their utmost to bring the persecuted to safety, carrying out an extremely dangerous mission, which exposed them to the risk of even losing their lives if discovered.

A large number of men of the Republican Police deployed extensive sabotage activities, managing to save hundreds of Jews, foreigners and Italians from death and deportation to Nazi camps.

An anthological account of the events that occurred is impossible, but by merely reporting a few examples, one will still get a picture of what effort was made by officers and ordinary agents of the Police Headquarters to save as many lives as possible.

Most famous remained the activities carried out by the penultimate Quaestor of Rijeka Giovanni Palatucci, remembered precisely as the "*Quaestor who helped the Jews.*" He enlisted in the Police in 1936 and transferred to the Rijeka Police Headquarters at the end of 1937, and in the following years he was appointed first Commissioner and later director of the foreigners' office. It was in this capacity that he came into direct contact with the harsh reality of the plight of Jews and did not leave Rijeka even when the Ministry ordered his transfer to Caserta in April 1939. His first major rescue operation was in March 1939, when he rescued some 800 fugitives, who were to be handed over to the Gestapo within hours. Palatucci alerted Rodolfo Grani, a Fiuman Jew, who obtained the intervention of Bishop Isidoro Sain, who temporarily hid the refugees in the nearby town of Abbazia, under the protection of the bishopric.

For his tireless work on behalf of Rijeka's Jews, which he continued with greater intensity after the Armistice, the police officer, who had been appointed Regent of the Questura in February, was arrested by the SS on Sept. 13, 1944, and taken to Trieste prison; from there he was transferred to the Dachau death camp on Oct. 22, dying there on Feb. 10, 1945, a few days before Liberation, at the age of only 36. In 1990, Yad Vashem in Jerusalem judged him "Righteous among the Nations," in 1995 the Italian state awarded him the Gold Medal of Civil Merit[35] and on March 21, 2000, the Vicariate of Rome sanctioned the opening of the process of beatification of the "Servant of God Giovanni Palatucci," which took place on October 9, 2002. In addition, at the ecumenical Jubilee ceremony on May 7, 2000, Pope John Paul II counted him among the martyrs of the 20th century.

In Rome, Commissioner Angelo De Fiore, head of the Foreigners Office, began helping Jews of non-Italian citizenship soon after the racial laws were passed. When the war broke out, he manipulated numerous files concerning Jews and suspected antifascist activity, thus hindering the Gestapo, which recalled him several times and put him under investigation, but without arriving at actual consequences. His activities were not limited to making false documents, with the help of Luigi Charrier, a clerk at the Registry Office, but he went so far as to carry out fake withdrawals

---

35 This is the motivation: "*Police officer, regent of the Rijeka Police Headquarters, did his utmost to help thousands of Jews and persecuted citizens, succeeding in preventing their arrest and deportation. Faithful to his commitment and although aware of the very grave personal risks he continued, despite the German occupation and the pressing incursions of Slavic partisans, his work as a leader, patriot and Christian, until his arrest by the Gestapo and his deportation to an extermination camp, where he sacrificed his young life.*"

from the city jails of Jews, passing them off as dangerous wanted men or deserters, releasing them soon after. After the Via Rasella bombing he was asked by his superior, Quaestor Pietro Caruso, to provide names of Jews on whom to carry out reprisals, and famous remained his reply, "I have no names of Jews to offer," with the excuse that the archives of the Office under his jurisdiction were not in order. There were no consequences for him and he was thus able to continue his work until the arrival of the Allies, when he went into hiding in fear of prosecution as a Police officer. He took care, however, to destroy and files of suspicious Jews and military personnel still in the archives of the Questura, with the help of his collaborators. Before the arrival of the Allies he actively collaborated with the clandestine group "Sprovieri" of the Military Clandestine Center, to which he communicated lists of politically persecuted and "undesirable" Italian officers. On July 8, 1969 he was recognized as a Righteous Among the Nations.

Some policemen of the Verona Police Headquarters, during the Social Republic, at the risk of their own lives, worked to save numerous Jews living in the city of Verona. The main protagonists in this affair, which enabled the Veronese community of about 300 Jews to pass the war substantially unscathed, were vice-brigadier Felice Sena, on the force of the Political Squad of the Verona Police Headquarters, and commissioners Guido Masiero and Antonino Gagliani. Only 34 Jews were arrested and sent to die in the concentration camps: they had all been taken by SS, Polizei or Fascist units, but not by units of the Questura scaligera. In fact, when Vice Brigadier Sena was forced to make an arrest to lead them to the Jewish concentration palace on Via Pallone, he never found any of the "wanted" people at home, except for the few who could not be arrested under the laws that provided for the release of those over seventy years old, those who had entered into mixed marriages or children who were the result of precisely mixed marriages. The studies of Veronese researcher Olinto Domenichini revealed that behind these sudden "disappearances" the three Veronese policemen were acting covertly: all of Sena's reports ended with the formula "*The searches have yielded negative results. It is reported that the same has left this city for unknown location since the ban on the concentration of members of the Jewish race. As for the seizure of property, the Jewish Property Administration Office provides. V. Brig. Sena Felice.*" Commissioners Gagliani and Masiero supported Sena's work and often themselves provided for the validation of false declarations of mixed marriages, effectively "freeing" Jews destined for deportation. Important was the help of physician Antonio Solli, who artfully created false certifications, and the parish priest of St. Euphemia, Don Marcello Chiampan, who documented the conversion to Catholicism, which in reality never took place, of some Jews. Also recently found was the written testimony of Deputy Commissioner Giuseppe Costantino, close to the Veronese Resistance, which confirms the presence of an organized group in the Questura headed by Masiero, a group that intensified its activity from the end of January 1944, when Gestapo Major Bosshammer arrived in the city and urged the Questura and Prefecture to do their duty in deporting Jews. Emblematic and little-known, on the other hand, are the exploits of the many officers, some of whom even sacrificed their own lives, as happened to Luigi Di Sano, who was killed by the Germans in Pisa on August 1, 1944. These men disobeyed their duties to the Laws of the Italian Social Republic out of humanity and common sense, thus becoming essential pawns in the partisan struggle, as in the case of the activity carried out by Agent Mario Canessa, on duty at the Tirano pass on the Swiss border during Operation "Diana," to rescue persecuted and prisoners. These were rescue operations, which distinguished race or religious beliefs. Canessa, during an interview, stated that he did not feel like a hero because of this, but simply said that "we *all did it or would have done it ... I just knew I had to help them.*"

These "non-heroes," Public Security Officers and Agents, acted spontaneously and non-organically throughout occupied Italy, obstructing files, generating confusion in Archives, hiding compromising documents within other files, destroying others and even fabricating false documents, such as ration cards and residence permits.

▲ Arditi of the Legione Autonoma Mobile 'Ettore muti' in a location in Piedmont (private collection Saronno).

▲ From left, Colonel Colombo, commander of the 'Muti' Legion, Minister Pavolini, commander of the Black Brigades, SS General Tensfeld and the Podestà of Milan, photographed on 28 October 1944, during a demonstration to commemorate the March on Rome (private collection Saronno).

▼ A group of Arditi of the 'Ettore Muti' in the summer of 1944 (private collection Saronno).

▲ Armed motorbike used by the 'Muti' Legion to patrol the Milan-Turin motorway.

▼ On 17 December 1944, Mussolini attended the parade of the 'Muti' Legion's units standing on one of the two L3 tanks of the 'Mezzi Pesanti' Company, in front of the Legion's headquarters in Via Rovello in Milan (the post-war building transformed into the famous 'Piccolo Teatro').

▲ A picture of the end: partisans in Milan occupied the barracks in Via Rovello, the headquarters of the 'Muti' Legion, now cleared of the Arditi. It is the morning of 26 April 1945. In front of the front door, an abandoned 'Del Buffa' motorcarriage is inspected with curiosity by partisans and police officers who have joined the Resistance (Pisanò archive).

▼ The trial of Renato Tartarotti, commander of the Special Autonomous Company, held in Bologna in 1945. Tartarotti is the first from the left, next to him on the stand, again from the left, other fascist defendants: Molmenti and the brothers Alberto and Paolo Gamberini.

▲ Mario Carità, in the centre of the photograph, portrayed with two elements of his band, the so-called Special Services Department.

▲ Pietro Koch, commander of the Special Republican Police Department, first active in Rome and, from June 1944, in Milan.

▲ Letterhead of the Special Republican Police Department, the notorious 'Koch Gang'.

▼ Pietro Koch was sentenced to death and shot on 5 June 1945 at Forte Bravetta in Rome.

▲▼ In the summer of 1944 Pietro Koch, began his ferocious and criminal activities at Villa Triste, formerly Villa Fossati in Milan. The place was apparently also frequented by the famous actor Osvaldo Valenti, but the accusation made against him by the partisans that he had taken part in the tortures inflicted by the Koch Gang on partisan prisoners turned out later to be completely fabricated, as later emerged before the Court of Appeal in Milan. Pictured above is the wall with plaques placed to commemorate the nefarious acts that occurred within those walls during the few months it was active.

▲ After the war almost all members of the criminal Carità gang were brought to trial before the Court of Assizes in Lucca in April 1951. Already after the Liberation, members of the gang were tried before the Extraordinary Court of Assizes in Padua: the trial ended on October 3, 1945. One of the members was sentenced to death and shot. After the Lucca trial, however, partly due to amnesty partly due to extraordinary events, almost all were released from prison

▼ The postwar trial of Guglielmo Blasi, one of the GAP members of Via Rasella, who was arrested by the fascists. In order to have his life saved, he betrayed his comrades by naming them and also passed into the service of the same gang. The Koch Gang thus succeeded in capturing and killing many members of the central GAP thanks to the former GAP member's confessions.

▲ Elements of the Special Auxiliary Police Department 'Tupin' of the Novara Police Headquarters in Valdossola in October 1944.

▼ A French truck carrying soldiers of the Special Auxiliary Police Department 'Tupin' in Domodossola.

UNIFORMS

The Republican Police officially adopted a new gray-green winter uniform to mark a marked departure from the previous Royal institutions even in the uniform. This new uniform consisted of a jacket of Saharan-like cut, without chest pockets, but with two large pockets with pointed tops on the hips and two slit pockets on the back. Long shawl pants, shirt and tie are used with this jacket. In addition, a coat with a closed, inverted collar is adopted, like the jacket, a shoulder reinforcement and uncovered button placket.

However, the distribution of these uniforms was only partially accomplished and, in fact, completed only in a few regional capitals, namely to the Auxiliary Battalions in the provinces of Milan, Genoa and Turin. For this reason, the most widespread uniform still remained the iron-gray uniform of the Corps of Public Security Officers, for which the stars were replaced with the gladiators of the Republican Armed Forces on the insignia and the crown and Savoy knot were eliminated from the frieze of the headgear and bandoleer. However, the introduction of the Republican friezes was met with discontent by most of the personnel of the Police Headquarters, who had enlisted before the fall of Fascism, and there were not a few cases of officers refusing to use the gladiolas. In contrast, the personnel of the Auxiliary Battalions and integrated only after the establishment of the Social Republic, welcomed the new uniformological provisions with enthusiasm,

With the old uniform the hard cap and pouch was worn; with the new uniform it was made compulsory to wear the pouch cap with visor, gray-green for the winter uniform, khaki for the summer uniform, and black for combat units.

The use of the gray-green helmet was also planned; a substantial proportion of policemen were equipped with Czechoslovak helmets, repainted gray-green or black over the original brown.

On the front of the cap was sewn a republican eagle, identical to that of the war flag of the Italian Social Republic. This frieze could be embroidered canutilla with gray-green or crimson cloth underneath, or in painted metal. The gold version was reserved for officers, and the silver version for all others.

The same eagle was applied to the front of the helmet in the form of a decal with a red background. On the left side of the same was sometimes a vertical tricolor shield, bordered in yellow and with the diagonal inscription "*HONOR.*"

The insignia were made of crimson cloth, in the shape of a parallelogram. On them was initially a fascet, later a circular wreath of oak leaves and a lictor's fascio were placed in place of the gladius, as the police depended on the Ministry of the Interior. Instead, battalions and special corps had a skull with a three-toothed dagger (silver in color) on the insignia.

A chest frieze was worn on the chest (above the right breast pocket), depicting an eagle with spread wings, holding a bundle in its talons. Above the eagle was the monogram *P.R.* (probably stood for "*Republican Police*").

Officers had rank badges on their counterparts, similar in shape to those of the M.V.S.N., but the rank designation was that of the Army. Marshals wore, also on the counter epaulettes, from one to three chevrons, arranged transversely; Brigadiers had two gold V chevrons on their sleeve, Deputy Brigadiers one, Chosen Guards two red rayon chevrons and Guards only one.

On April 10, 1945, a circular prescribed the summer uniform, in khaki cloth, consisting of safari jacket, shirt and shawl pants. With both uniforms the leather belt, without shoulder strap, with holster for the gun was to be worn (both the jacket and coat had two loops at the hips to support it).

Throughout the war period Army uniforms (jackets with and without lapels, long or cavalry-style pants) were also worn at the same time, especially by the Arditi and combat units.

Police Armed Forces Legion "Pietro Caruso"

The crimson insignia proper to the Police were worn in the shape of a parallelogram, with a frieze consisting of a laurel and oak wreath, surmounted by a lictor's fasces, to which was superimposed a skull with crossed shinbones, all made of war metal. In some photos and in the postcard edited for the Legion, some militiamen, but mostly officers, are seen wearing two-pronged flames, divided diagonally in half; the upper part was crimson, the lower black, with the metal frieze described above (sometimes without the skullcap).

On the cap was sewn a frieze similar to that of other Public Security corps, an eagle with a dagger (instead of a bundle) in its talons. It could be made of metal or canutile (gold for officers, silver for others), embroidered on gray-green cloth.

There are no indications regarding the friezes on the helmet, but, presumably, they were like those adopted for the other Public Security corps, although in one photograph, attributable to the "Caruso" Legion, a frieze, made with decalcomania or painted, replicating the chest badge of the Republican Police, can be seen on the left side of the helmet.

An Ardito badge to be worn on the arm was also made for Legion members, identical to that of the Army, except for the stand, which was made of crimson cloth instead of gray-green.

Finally, it would appear that the Arditi wore a strange beret with a visor, made of gray-green cloth, with a red and black cord and the Police eagle as a frieze. At least one specimen of this headgear exists, although there is no photographic evidence to prove its actual use by the department's militiamen.

Special Inspectorate of Anti-Partisan Police

Members of the assault units of the I.S.P.A. had on their crimson insignia the oak leaf wreath with the bundle, as for other P.S. departments, but with the bundle in red, with a skull with crossed shinbones in the center.

Members of the Mobile Assault Units had sewn on their left sleeve a metal shield painted black, with a silver border. In the center of it was depicted the fascio littorio in red with a skullcap, at the foot of which was the acronym "I.S.P.A." (without an endpoint!) and two crossed daggers. Along the three straight sides of the shield was the inscription "*NUCLEO/ MOBILE/ D'ASSALTO.*" All inscriptions were silver in color. It is unclear whether a fabric version of this shield was also made.

Autonomous Mobile Legion "Ettore Muti"

The typical Legion uniform was depicted on Coscia's famous poster for enlistment in the Muti. It consisted of a paratrooper's jacket and gray-green shawl pants (in a few photographs one sees militiamen also wearing below-the-knee shorts with gray-green socks), a black shirt or turtleneck sweater. A brown leather belt with a gold buckle was worn over the vest. Protective clothing could be worn, such as gray-green windbreakers, the type also used by the Bersaglieri, gray-green cloth coats and brown leather jackets by officers.

In the summer, the uniform did not vary, except that no vest was worn; however, legionnaires with a khaki Saharan vest are noted.

The skiers wore, in addition to their normal clothing, a white camouflage suit consisting of long pants and reversible German camouflage jacket (white on one side, mouse gray on the other). Carristians wore both the Legion's own uniform and the turquoise jumpsuit and black leather tank jacket.

The standard headgear was the gray-green beret, for all Legion members. In rare cases one sees militiamen wearing the gray-green envelope cap, but these are exceptions. In addition to the beret, the use of the gray-green M33 helmet, devoid of any frieze, was prescribed. Carristians also wore black leather helmets.

The department's insignia were black pentagonal, charged with a red fascet on the top (similar to that used by the Black Brigades) and a skull with crossed shinbones on the bottom.

A shield with the Legion's symbol was sewn on the left sleeve of the leather jacket, coat, or vest. The shield was made of metal painted blue for the troop and of blue or blue cloth with gold canvass embroidery for officers. It was often sewn above the left breast pocket of the vest. On it was the Legion's coat of arms, consisting of a republican fasces with two crossed daggers; at the bottom was the inscription: "*AUTONOMOUS MOBILE LEGION - E. MUTI - MILAN.*"

Badges of various designs, especially skulls with crossed shinbones, or rank badges (those of the Army), were often worn above the left sleeve of the vest, which were instead to be worn on the left sleeve by graduates. On the left sleeve or above the left pocket of the vest many militiamen had the Ardito badge. Above the left breast pocket of the black shirt was embroidered in red the name of the Legion, inside a box, also red.

A separate discussion deserves the windbreaker jacket. On it the badge was applied on the front, above the left pocket; in the same place were sewn the badges of rank, both by officers and graduates, or the badge of the Arditi.

The frieze of the headgear consisted of a large skull with metallic crossed shinbones; officers wore instead a canutile wire frieze composed of golden oak and laurel branches, with a black roundel, in the center of which was the usual skullcap. On the left side of the beret it was customary to have rank badges.

Legionnaires engaged in public order duties wore a white cloth armband with black borders and with the inscription, also in black, "*LEGION AUTONOMA MUTI - POLIZEI.*" All legionnaires were given a war metal bracelet with a plaque, on which was depicted

Finally, the (limited) use of the gold plaque for the belt, representing the department's coat of arms (Fascio littorio with crossed daggers and the motto, in italics, "*Siam fatta così*" (*We are made like this*), is worth mentioning.

▲ A member of the Reparto d'Assalto della Polizia (R.A.P.) in Bologna, photographed in 1944. Interesting is the use of the beret, a unique case in the panorama of the Republican police (if we exclude the 'Ettore Muti' Legion).

▼ Elements of the Special Inspectorate of Public Security for Venezia Giulia, photographed together with a German soldier. In the centre, identified by the number 5 and an arrow, is Deputy Commissioner Gaetano Collotti, from whose name the unit was named 'Banda Collotti'.

▲ Republican police officer with embroidered insignia of the first type, with fasces without laurel wreath.

▲ Model 40 jacket of a Republican Police officer (WEB source).

▲ Captain's hat of the Republican Police; this is probably a garment made in the first months of the Italian Social Republic, because the cap frieze is made on grey-green cloth and not on the regular crimson cloth (Riccardo Pantanelli collection).

▼ Special Battalions insignia of the Republican Police (Riccardo Pantanelli collection).

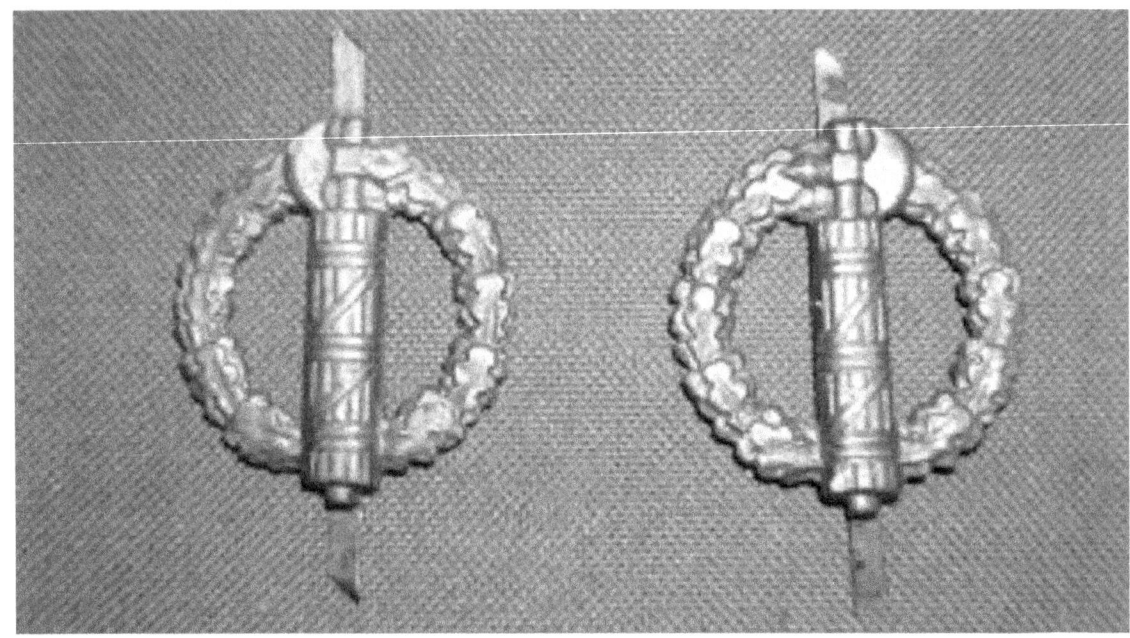

▲ Republican Police Badge (Riccardo Pantanelli Collection).

▼ Republican Police officer's cap frieze in canutilla embroidered on crimson cloth (WEB source).

▲ Set of Republican Police friezes, consisting of the chest frieze, in the very rare metal version, silver-plated cap frieze and a pair of insignia charged with the Republican fasces (Uguccioni Collections).

▼ The Police Armed Forces Legion 'Pietro Caruso' armband badge, identical in spelling to that of the Army, but made on crimson cloth. This is a modern reproduction (WEB source).

▲ Poor quality reproduction of the metal badge of the Nuclei Mobili d'Assalto of the Ispettorato Speciale Polizia Anti Partigiani (WEB source).

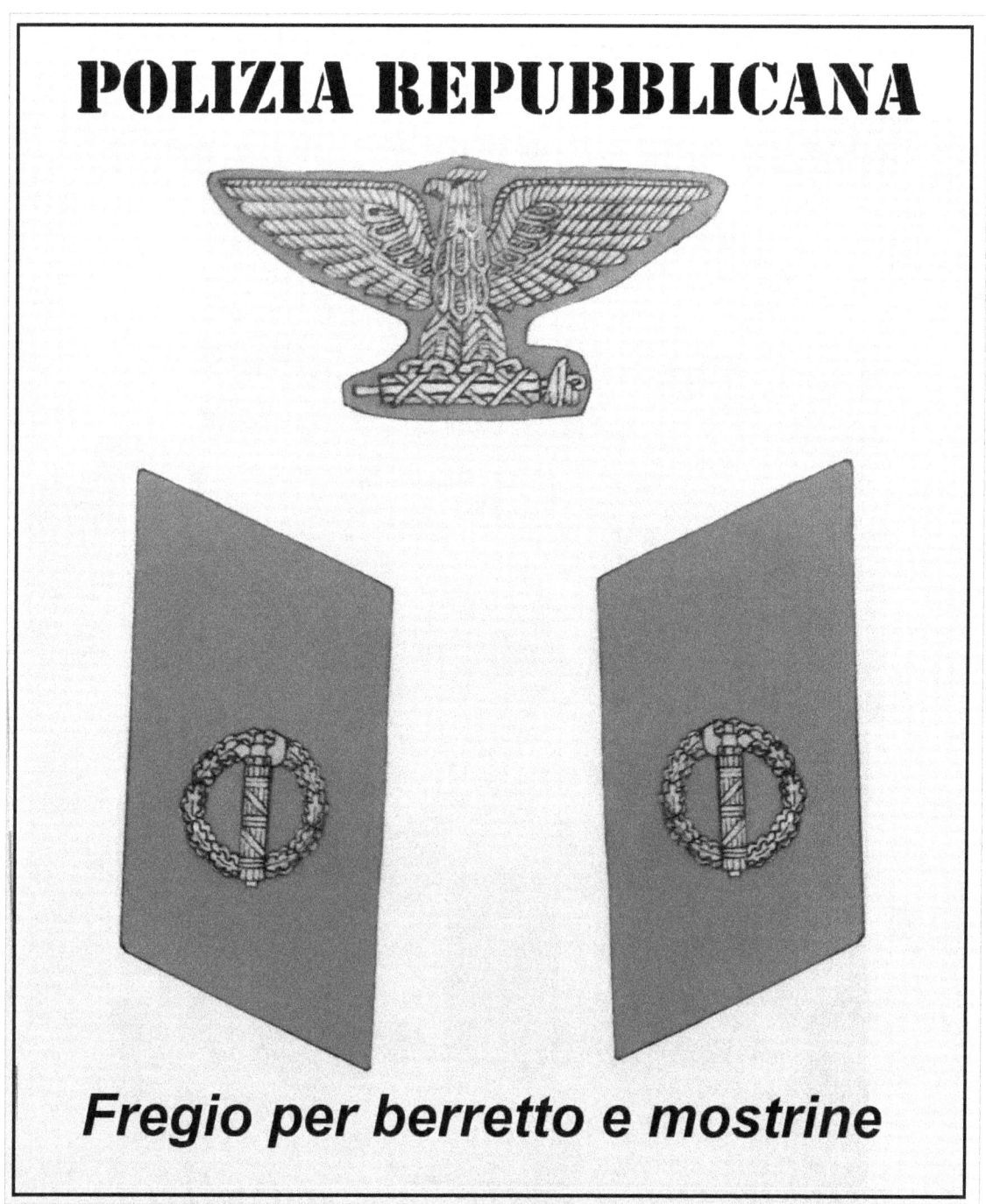

▲ Riproduzione delle mostrine e del fregio della Polizia repubblicana R.S.I.

▲ Reproduction of the insignia and cap frieze of the Police Arditi Legion "Pietro Caruso" of the Republican Police R.S.I.

BIBLIOGRAPHY

BOOKS

- Arena Nino, "L'Italia in guerra 1940/45", Ermanno Albertelli Editore, Parma, 1997.
- Arena Nino, "R.S.I. – Forze Armate della Repubblica Sociale – La guerra in Italia – 1943 – 1944 – 1945", Ermanno Albertelli Editore, Parma, 2002.
- Arena Nino, "Soli contro tutti", Edizioni Ultima Crociata, Milano, 1993.
- Balugani Ronaldo, "La scia di sangue lasciata dai Tupin (1943-1945)", Edizioni Sigem, Modena, 1999.
- Caporale Riccardo, "La "Banda Carità". Storia del Reparto Servizi Speciali (1943-45)", Edizioni San Marco Litotipo, Lucca, 2004.
- Corbatti Sergio, Nava Marco, "…come il diamante!", Laran Editions, Bruxelles 2008.
- Crippa Paolo, "I mezzi corazzati della Guerra Civile 43 -45", Mattioli 1885, Parma, 2015.
- Crippa Paolo, "Italia 43 – 45 – I blindati di circostanza della Guerra Civile", Mattioli 1885, Parma, 2014.
- Cucut Carlo, "Le Forze Armate della R.S.I. 1943 – 1945 – Forze di Terra", G.M.T., Trento, 2005.
- Cucut Carlo, "Le Forze Armate della R.S.I. sul confine orientale – settembre 1943 – maggio 1945", Marvia Edizioni, Voghera (PV), 2009.
- Domenichini Olinto, "Le ricerche hanno dato esito negativo. I giusti della Questura e le persecuzioni razziali a Verona (1943-1945)", Cierre Edizioni, Caselle (VR), 2021.
- Fazzo Luca, "L'ultimo fucilato", Mursia, Milano, 2015.
- Griner Massimiliano, "La "banda Koch". Il reparto speciale di polizia 1943-44", Torino, Bollati Boringhieri, 2000.
- Guglielmi Daniele, Tallillo Andrea, Tallillo Antonio, "CarriL3. Carri Veloci, Carri leggeri, derivati", G.M.T., Trento, 2004.
- Kuchler Heinz, "Fregi, mostrine e distintivi della R.S.I.", Intergest, Milano, 1974.
- Marzetti Paolo, "Uniformi e distintivi italiani 1933 – 1945", Ermanno Albertelli Editore, Parma 1995.
- Memo Giovanni, "La banda Koch a Milano. Tra i reclusi a "Villa Triste", Tipografia Editoriale Luigi Memo, Milano, 1945 link a pdf
- Oliva Gianni, "L'ombra nera, Le stragi nazifasciste che non ricordiamo più", Arnoldo Mondadori Editore, Milano, 2007.
- Pisanò Giorgio, "Gli ultimi in grigioverde", Edizioni F.P.E., Milano 1967.
- Pisanò Giorgio, "Storia della Guerra Civile in Italia", Edizioni F.P.E., Milano 1967.
- Rosignoli Guido, "R.S.I. Uniformi, distintivi, equipaggiamenti e armi 1943-45", Ermanno Albertelli Editore, Parma, 1998.
- Sparacino Fausto, "Distintivi e medaglie della R.S.I., della Legione S.S. Italiana, dei Veterani della R.S.I." E.M.I., Milano, 1998.
- Sparacino Fausto, "Distintivi e medaglie della R.S.I." E.M.I., Milano, 1994.

Magazines

- "Acta" della Fondazione R.S.I. – Istituto Storico, Terranuova Bracciolini (AR), numeri vari.
- "Il generale Montagna costituisce la Legione Arditi della Polizia "P. Caruso"" ne "il Popolo del Friuli", 27 novembre 1944.
- Adami Maria Vittoria, "Verona, i giusti della Questura" ne "L'Arena", 26 gennaio 2021.
- Lombardo Mario, "La Repubblica di Salò", in Storia Illustrata n°200, Arnoldo Mondadori Editore, Milano, luglio 1974.
- Pisani Marco, Tagliazucchi Enrico, "Il Reparto Speciale di Pietro Koch: la Banda Koch", in "Fronti di guerra", n° 90, novembre – dicembre 2023.
- Poggiali Luca, "La Polizia Repubblicana nella R.S.I.", in "Storia e Battaglie, n° 240, novembre – dicembre 2022.
- Puleio Nino, "Quell'aprile a Milano", ne "Avanti!", 25 aprile 1967.
- Stagno Raffaele, "La Polizia Repubblicana", in "Fiamme d'Oro, anno XLVII – numero 2, maggio – agosto 2020.

Other documents

- Calore Gianmarco, "Polizia Repubblicana e Agenti di Pubblica Sicurezza: cenni storici sul passaggio istituzionale".
- Mattinali delle Questure Repubblicane di Milano, Torino, Genova, Bologna, Venezia, Vercelli, Cuneo, Varese, conservati presso i rispettivi Archivi di Stato.
- Notiziari della Guardia Nazionale Repubblicana.
- Bollettino Ufficiale del Ministero dell'Interno.
- Bollettino Ufficiale del Corpo delle Guardie di Pubblica Sicurezza (anno 1945 e seguenti).
- Archivio Storico di Cuneo, annuari 1944, 1945 e 1946.
- Testimonianza dell'Appuntato Agostino Bernardi.
- Testimonianza del Maresciallo Arcangelo Stiuso.

TITOLI GIÀ PUBBLICATI - TITLES ALREADY PUBLISHING

TITOLI GIÀ PUBBLICATI - TITLES ALREADY PUBLISHING

BOOKS TO COLLECT

www.ingramcontent.com/pod-product-compliance
Lightning Source LLC
LaVergne TN
LVHW081452060526
838201LV00050BA/1779